SHINTO

The Way of Japan

SHINTO

The Way of Japan

by Floyd Hiatt Ross

GREENWOOD PRESS, PUBLISHERS
WESTPORT, CONNECTICUT

Library of Congress Cataloging in Publication Data

Ross, Floyd Hiatt.
  Shinto, the way of Japan.

    Reprint. Originally published: Boston : Beacon Press,
  1965.
      Bibliography: p.
      Includes index.
      1. Shinto. I. Title.
  BL2220.R6 1983   299'.561   83-12970
  ISBN 0-313-24240-2 (lib. bdg.)

Photographs supplied through the courtesy of the Jinja Honcho (Shrine Association) in Tokyo.

The author gratefully acknowledges permission to reprint passages from *Norito*, translated by D. Philippi (published by Kokugakuin University, Shibuya, Tokyo, 1959); *Kokutai-no Hongi*, edited by Robert King Hall, translated by John Owen Gauntlett (Harvard University Press, Cambridge, Mass., 1949).

In romanization of Japanese words, long marks are not shown on common terms and names such as Shinto, Tokyo, Kyoto, Kato, etc., unless they appear in quotations. The Hepburn system of romanization has been followed.

Reprinted in 1983 by Greenwood Press
A division of Congressional Information Service, Inc.
88 Post Road West, Westport, Connecticut 06881

Printed in the United States of America

10 9 8 7 6 5 4 3 2 1

To David and Bruce

Acknowledgments

This does not pretend to be a volume for Japanese specialists. It is intended to fill a gap that the specialists, engrossed in the details of their own pursuits, have overlooked. I wish to express appreciation to the officials and faculty of Kokugakuin University, and to President Yukitada Sasaki, who is also president of the Institute for Japanese Culture and Classics, for the many courtesies extended to me during my stay there. My indebtedness to Professor Hatsuo Tanaka is very great, for his guidance on the many trips to shrines, and for the two evenings a week he gave me out of his busy schedule. With his daughter, Kashihi Tanaka, a Japanese edition of this book is being prepared. Professor Naofusa Hirai was gracious enough to make valuable suggestions in connection with the chapter "Shinto Ideas of *Kami*," and Mr. William Woodard read three of the last chapters of the book. To my wife goes thanks for the tedious job of proofreading.

If there are mistakes in my presentation which might distort the overall picture of Shinto, I assume responsibility for them and would appreciate correspondence concerning them. I trust the main purpose of the book will not be lost sight of—to increase the areas of understanding between the people of two differing cultures with reference to man's search for meaningful relatedness.

Preface

Since the end of World War II the West has "discovered" Japan anew, with great enthusiasm, and a search is underway aimed at finding out what Japan is or is like. In this process many Japans have been discovered. There is the Japan which still nurses the psychological wounds resulting from the nation's defeat. There is the Japan which still boasts of its ancient culture while rushing to imitate the fads and fashions of the West. There is also the young Japan that seems to want to turn its back on most of its cultural heritage in the process of aping the West. There is the Japan of the extreme right wing with its sometimes sinister organizations which attract individuals ready to take "direct action" after the fashion of some of the loyalists before the imperial restoration in 1868, or in the style of the fanatical patriots of the 1930's. The young naval officers and army cadets who assassinated Premier Inukai on May 15, 1932, claimed they were attempting to free the emperor from evil advisers. Such men were influenced by the propaganda of the ultra-nationalistic societies.

There is also the Japan of the left wing, occasionally quite vociferous, sometimes asking for the total elimination of the emperor system and the acceptance of Marxist modes of thinking and action. There is the Japan of the students who work hard to pass the examinations that will allow them to enter the "right" university and who, once admitted, spend much of their time loafing. There is also the Japan of the mad scramble for status, position, advancement on the hierarchical ladder, and the privilege of being near the centers of power in Tokyo. There is rural Japan, which is steadily losing its population to the great urban centers.

But which Japan is the fundamental one? If one's objective is to understand the Japanese people themselves in their cultures, one must try to discover what lies deep within the Japanese mind and heart, deeper than the westernization and the modernization. It is too easy to be misled by the outer changes. A casual tourist view of the country could lead the visitor to conclude that the Japanese have abandoned their past, their myths and legends, their traditions, their mixed feelings of cultural superiority and inferiority.

This mistake of not looking below the surface was made by many Western writers decades ago when they wrote that Buddhism was much more important in the tradition and life of Japan than Shinto. It is true that Buddhism has been a potent force in the life of Japan through the centuries. Over a generation ago Lafcadio Hearn wrote:

> All that can be classed under the name of art in Japan was either introduced or developed by Buddhism; and the same may be said regarding nearly all Japanese literature possessing real literary quality— excepting some Shinto rituals, and some fragments of archaic poetry. Buddhism introduced drama, the higher forms of poetical composition, and fiction, and history, and philosophy. All the refinements of Japanese life were of Buddhist introduction, and at least a majority of its diversions and pleasures. . . . Buddhism brought the whole of Chinese civilization into Japan, and thereafter patiently modified and reshaped it to Japanese requirements. The elder civilization was not merely superimposed upon the social structure, but fitted carefully into it, combined with it so perfectly that the marks of the welding, the lines of the juncture, almost totally disappeared.*

Hearn added, much later in the same book, that "though Buddhism did for a long period appear to have almost entirely absorbed Shinto, by the acknowledgment of the Shinto scholars themselves, though Buddhist emperors reigned who neglected or despised the cult of their ancestors; though Buddhism directed, during ten centuries, the education of the nation, Shinto remained all the while so very much alive that it was able not only to dispossess its rival at last, but to save the country from foreign domination."†

Buddhism has been an influence in the life of Japan, a very

---

* Lafcadio Hearn, *Japan: An Attempt at an Interpretation* (New York: The Macmillan Company, 1928), pp. 224-225.
† *Ibid.*, p. 413.

strong influence. But Shinto is more than an influence. It is the vital, pervasive way in which the Japanese have taken hold of life at the fundamental level of their being, and I would suggest that it is still the most authentic expression of their basic attitude toward life. This holds true in spite of the agnosticism and modernization which are so readily apparent to any person who lives among the Japanese for a while. To prove this hypothesis is, of course, impossible. But the following chapters represent an attempt to make this claim regarding Shinto in the way of the Japanese a "probable account." We should take seriously what the Japanese themselves seem to take seriously at the subconscious level of their lives, even when they often refuse to take it seriously at the conscious level.

This book is not a study of "Folk Shinto," that is, of those numerous attitudes and practices associated with the life of the peasants and villagers, including many practices and superstitions that go back for centuries but which have never been incorporated into the main festivals of "Shrine Shinto." Only a few aspects of "Folk Shinto" are mentioned in these pages. It impinges upon "Shrine Shinto" at many points but is not central to it.

What is still often referred to as "Sect Shinto" is not dealt with in these pages. This term came into use in the Meiji period near the end of the nineteenth century, to label thirteen religious groups which had legal status with the Japanese government and which from 1900 until 1945 were under the jurisdiction of the "Office of Religions" in the national government. The founders of several of these sects claimed special revelations and many of their teachings have no vital connection with the main currents of Shinto myth or practice. Since 1945, several of these groups refuse to accept the label of "Shinto," and it is misleading for modern writers to go on referring to them as though they were part of the main stream of Shinto.

The Shinto which we shall concentrate on is a relatively formless tradition of ancient festivals and feelings much older than the term "Shinto," which came into being after the great influx of Chinese religions and philosophies. When the very early periods of this Japanese tradition are referred to, it is called by many writers "Ancient Shinto." Since World War II it has commonly been called "Shrine Shinto," which distinguishes it from that "national Shinto" or "state Shinto" which was made into the national faith of Japan by government regulation by the opening of the twentieth century. Most of the important Shinto shrines in Japan today belong to a "Shrine Association" (*Jinja Honchō*). Hence the appropriateness of the name "Shrine Shinto."

Today in Japan one can soon discover that most young people know very little about Shinto in its traditional forms, but the *force* of Shinto is there just the same, below the surface. In 1964, during the three days of the New Year's holidays, visitors to the nation's Shinto shrines and Buddhist temples set a postwar record of 20,274,900 according to the Police Agency. How many of these visitors were truly pilgrims it is of course impossible to say. But consider just the few following examples of the number of visitors to key Shinto shrines.

Meiji Shrine, in Tokyo	1,045,000	visitors
Sumiyoshi Shrine, in Osaka	1,092,000	visitors
Toyokawa Inari Shrine, Aichi	831,000	visitors
Fushimi Inari Shrine, in Kyoto	800,000	visitors
Ise Grand Shrine	788,000	visitors
Atsuta Shrine, Aichi	580,000	visitors

When one stops to realize that Ise Grand Shrine is not near a large metropolitan center, the figure is indeed astounding. The total number of visitors to the shrines on which the police kept accounts showed an increase of nearly three million over last year. During the past few years I have visited scores of Shinto shrines myself. Consistently the priests have reported, with only two or three exceptions, that each year finds more people coming to the shrines throughout the course of the year. Some of this they admit is traceable to the Japanese love of sightseeing. What other factors may be at work in the Japanese heart they do not profess to know. Many of the visitors are unable to express their reasons for visiting the shrines, even when they are asked.

The street in front of Miyajidake Jinja (Kyūshū region.)

The annual festival of a shrine is usually the most important event as far as the number of people in attendance is concerned. Each shrine has its own date and its own special traditions. The one pictured here is in the Tōhoku region, and includes the usual procession with portable shrine.

A decade ago James Clark Moloney, a doctor, wrote a book called *Understanding the Japanese Mind,* in which he stated his conviction that the Japanese are neither "mysterious," "inscrutable," nor "unpredictable." They are, he wrote, "entirely reasonable, understandable, and predictable when one understands fully the restrictions which have been placed upon their behavior, individual and collective, by the traditions of the ages."‡ This is a fairly rash statement with which I am not prepared to agree, for I do not have that much confidence in the findings of the social sciences, including the field of psychiatry in which Dr. Moloney works. I am not unaware of the restrictive, or negative, features in the Japanese culture, features upon which his book tends to focus. But there is much of value in the traditional Japanese way of viewing life and of living it. What are the factors that have enabled a people like the Japanese to pass through, in a few generations, what Europe took several centuries to go through? And they have passed through it fairly successfully. In the process they experienced a catastrophe such as they had never known in the history of their land. That catastrophe—the defeat of their nation and the consequent loss of faith in themselves and their leadership—did not overwhelm them as a people. Such a culture and its people deserve high respect as well as study.

How does one get hold of those underlying dimensions which are usually by-passed in a culture by the more quantitatively-oriented studies made by those who rely heavily upon statistical methods and an intense study of one small segment of a society? Granting the greater accuracy of a photographic reproduction (if one is thinking of the external aspects of the situation only), is there also a value in the painting which is done with broader strokes and on a larger scale, especially if it is human mood, feelings, and value-nuances that are sought? The two types of approaches must seek to remain in touch with each other, but each approach has something to contribute to an understanding of the total situation.

---

‡ James Clark Moloney, *Understanding the Japanese Mind* (Tokyo: Charles E. Tuttle Co., Inc., 1954).

My own approach includes personal involvement in part of the life of Shinto through participation in festivals, conversations with many Shinto priests and scholars, and a year in a Shinto University. In this book we shall look at some of the activities and ideas of Shinto, including its myths, trying to discover something of what they have meant to the Japanese themselves.

F. H. R.

October, 1964

Contents

SHINTO

The Way of Japan

CHAPTER ONE

Visit to a Shinto Shrine

The non-rational forces in a society or culture are under-estimated more frequently by the scholar than by the politician. Much of the life of religion and art falls outside the systematic analyses that intellectuals like to devise. Shrewd politicians in all ages have known how to make use of religion for their own purposes, using myths, religious legends, and rituals freely to further their own or their tribal purposes. Sociologists and psychologists of religion often content themselves largely with the process of describing religious behavior, using the current standards of "objectivity" within the area of their specialization. Theologians have a natural tendency to talk about religion with reference to beliefs or doctrines which they desire to propound or defend and, like many scholars of religion, allow an alleged "objectivity" to screen out whatever they cannot handle in the other culture's religion. And, since Marx, many study religion only to show how it will "wither away" with the right kind of education and proper control of the basic means of production.

But much of the life of mankind is lived below the level of neat conceptual formulas. This is especially true when one tries to study something as non-organized and non-conceptualized as Japanese Shinto. For example, to start a discussion of Shinto with one of the usual Western questions, "What is religion?" would not take us very far. For Japan, as for many Oriental cultures, religion has been *a way of walking* or living, not a belief or a theory to be philosophically expounded. If a Japanese does "think" about religion, he is inclined to think in terms of peace of mind or serenity of spirit. By contrast, a Christian or a Moslem is inclined to think in terms of whether one "believes in God" or in "the decrees of Allah," or possibly belief in the Bible or the Koran. There is a vast difference between these two ways of taking hold of religion or discussing it, and Westerners too often ignore it.

We shall proceed by a different method, looking first at the rituals and myths of Shinto, then examining some of the ideas and feelings associated with them, trying to discover something of what they mean to the Japanese, even to those who claim to have no religion at all. Certainly agnosticism as known in the West is widespread among the Japanese, as also is the notion that the Japanese people are the most irreligious people on the planet. Yet even though many may deny it verbally, certain ways of feeling about themselves, about nature and their relation to it, about their myths and legends, still play an important part in the lives of the Japanese. Let us begin with a visit to a Shinto shrine.

Our bus, so crowded that there was barely room to keep both feet on the floorboards, wound slowly along narrow country roads in the province of Shizuoka. We had ridden for several hours on an express train, standing up all the way, from Tokyo Station to the town of Fukuroi. Not too long before, we had passed through Shizuoka City. If we had stayed on the train a few more stations, we would have come to Hamamatsu, near Hamana Lake, an inlet off the Pacific Ocean and a spot visited by many Japanese tourists. But our destination was a Shinto shrine named Sakura-ga-ike-miya. We could have left the train at any of three towns, Kikugawa, Kakegawa, or Fukuroi. We choose Fukuroi. We could have taken a local train to the town of Sakura-ga-ike, but that would have consumed another two hours, and the buses went directly to the shrine in only fifty minutes.

Even the bus ride was quite slow. The bus was unimaginably overloaded and the scent of human passengers was over-strong. Practically all of the people on our bus—as on the scores of others we were soon to see—were pilgrims or sightseers on their way to this one shrine on the occasion of its three-day annual festival. As our bus approached the area of the shrine, it was apparent that scores of special buses arriving ahead of ours had taken up about all of the limited space available for parking at the edge of the fields. Our progress was finally completely blocked by the traffic jam and the driver allowed us to get off about half a mile from the shrine.

We found ourselves with thousands of others, walking along a narrow gravel road which in most places was not wide enough to allow the returning buses to drive past the buses which were still arriving with more people. Policemen with walkie-talkies were making almost vain efforts to keep the pedestrians and the buses moving. In spite of the crowding, most everyone seemed to be in good spirits though the day was a hot one. The great majority of the people around us seemed to be country folk, to judge from their clothing, their hands and their faces. Some, however, had the appearance of city dwellers. In the crowds immediately around me, I was unable to see any other foreigner. In recent years this three-day event had drawn more than 100,000 visitors. It is estimated that perhaps as many as 50 per cent of the people are women from farming villages within the surrounding area, returning to the festival faithfully every year. The festival begins on the autumn equinox, which happens also to be the day of one of the very popular semi-annual Buddhist festivals called the Paramita service. These people crowding around me into a Shinto shrine were Japanese, alleged by many to be uninterested in religion. Yet where in the United States, a country supposed to be "religious," could one have found one hundred thousand people turning out for a purely religious festival?

Half of the crowd along the road was trying to make its way out of the shrine precincts while the other half struggled good-naturedly to make its way in. Up the long winding lane toward the main shrine we walked. There were the usual food stalls and small souvenir stands set up along the path. These sought the attention of adults as well as children and made the flow of traffic even slower. Loudspeakers were mounted on poles along the route, and from time to time they blared forth some announcement or urged the crowds not to push and shove.

The mood of the crowd was not one of solemnity or reverence, it seemed. Everyone was enjoying a good time. It might have been a crowd going to a county fair. Near the main shrine worship hall and shrine office, the crowd became even denser. An atmosphere of expectation could be sensed. Many were moving in the direction of the small lake or pond around whose edge, about fifty feet back from the shore, a temporary fence had been erected. This consisted of canvas strung along on bamboo poles. By paying a small fee one was allowed to pass to the other side of the bamboo curtain where it was possible to have a closer view of the special rituals being performed on the pond. A tall foreigner could look over the fence and since there seemed to be no more space inside the enclosure for our presence, we contented ourselves with peering over the top of the canvas.

Between the fence and the shore of the pond thousands of people stood jammed closely together. They were intently watching the activities taking place out on the pond. A boat in which white-robed Shinto priests were standing was being slowly rowed around by young men naked except for loincloths. In the pond other young men were treading water while holding on to round, covered boxes which they were twirling around.

What manner of festival was this? That this was a Shinto shrine was evidenced by the white attire of the priests in the boat. In addition, on our way to the pond all of us had passed through a large Shinto *torii* or shrine gateway, and we had stopped at a purification place to rinse our mouths with water and to wash our hands before proceeding to the inner precincts of the shrine. However, this particular annual festival includes elements drawn from ancient folk belief, popular piety flavored with Buddhism of the Pure Land sect (*Jōdo-shū*), and traditional Shrine Shinto.

The main *kami* or divinity enshrined here is a *kami* charged with the function of purification.* There are also two subordinate *kami* at this shrine, one of whom is the main *kami* at Suwa Shrine

---

* On the impossibility of an adequate translation of the term *kami*, see Chapter Three. The term *divinity* is sufficiently vague for the first occurrence of this word. Hereafter, it will be left untranslated except when other authors are being quoted directly.

many miles away in another prefecture. This pond, called Sakura-ga-ike, is supposed to have no bottom and is connected, so it has been believed, with Lake Suwa, on whose shores the Suwa Shrine stands.[1] According to the local tradition at Sakura-ga-ike Shrine, many years ago a female *kami* named Seoritsu-hime-no-kami, appeared to the governor of this locale and requested him to build a shrine for her at this spot. Formerly there were two ponds at this site, one considered male and the other female. A long time ago the male pond disappeared. Now only a muddy spot reminds the visitor of where it used to be. While the male pond used to be the center of the belief, after its water disappeared, the female pond name Sakura-ga-ike became the center of religious practices.

Within the precincts of this Shinto shrine there is also a Buddhist temple, Sakura-no-miya.[2] A Buddhist monk named Kōen is enshrined in this temple. Kōen was a famous monk and scholar of the Tendai school of Buddhism. He was a teacher of Hōnen (1133-1212), the founder of the Pure Land sect of Buddhism. It is very unusual for a Buddhist monk to be enshrined within the precincts of a Shinto shrine, but there is a legend explaining this. Though Kōen was a great scholar, he was not able to reach enlightenment or Nirvana. He became acutely aware of this shortly before his death, and it caused him considerable anxiety. He was acquainted with the Buddhist story concerning the coming of Miroku Bosatsu at the end of the world. At that time all living things would be saved. This event was supposed to take place over five billion years after the death of the Buddha. Kōen wanted to be present on that great occasion so he would be among the living things which would be saved. This meant he had to find some way of staying alive until that time. He decided to become a dragon, since a dragon lives longer than any other creature.

In that ancient time it was said that the pond of Sakura reached all the way to the palace of the Dragon Under the Sea. Thus Kōen made up his mind to live as a dragon in this pond. When he lay near death on Mount Hiei, the center of the Tendai sect of Buddhism just outside of Kyoto, he asked that some water from the pond of Sakura be brought to him. Looking into this

water and seeing his own reflection on the surface, he died peace-
fully, believing that from then on he would live as a dragon in
the pond, waiting for the eventual salvation promised through
Miroku Bosatsu.

Long before the present Shinto shrine was erected and dedicated to the *kami* of purification, there was a Dragon Shrine for
the worship of this Dragon Kami. Since this Dragon Kami was
considered very mysterious and awesome, when people had to
go near the pond to get water for irrigation purposes, they went
in for strict measures of purification at the shrine of the *kami*
of purification. As the years passed, however, people seemed to
lose some of their dread of the Dragon Kami. The result was that
the *kami* of purification became increasingly important. By the
time the legend about Kōen had made its appearance, belief in
the original dragon had died out. Hence, on the occasion of the
annual festival when boxes of rice are sent to the bottom of the
pond, it is Kōen as the dragon who is presumably being fed.

I looked again at the young men swimming in the pond, each
twirling his round box filled with rice. These men had been selected from the young men of good reputation in the *uji-ko*, families
belonging to the shrine. Usually about a dozen are chosen. Prior
to the festival they go through a purification period of seven days
and nights in a special section of the chief priest's residence. During this period they are cut off from all contact with the everyday
activities of the outside world. Their meals are cooked on a sacred
fire which is not used for ordinary cooking. Each day, as soon as
they get up they undergo purification in cold well-water and then
go to the shrine for worship. After that is concluded, they walk
about a mile to the seashore and purify themselves in salt water.
They go under the waves seventy-five times. On the evening of
each day they repeat these purification rites.

These young men also assist in preparing the rice which is
used in the festival. A fire is started by twirling a stick rapidly
in a board with a small hole. The rice for the offerings to be made
during the festival is cooked over this fire and is then placed in
boxes which are about one foot in diameter and about nine inches

Each year the young men chosen to participate in the annual festival go through various purifications for seven days. In the morning and in the evening of each day, they go under the waves seventy-five times. Purification by sea water is a very ancient practice.

The young men at Sakura-ga-ike Shrine help prepare the cooked rice, which is placed in the boxes, with five strips of paper attached to a stick (a *go-hei*) put on top of the rice.

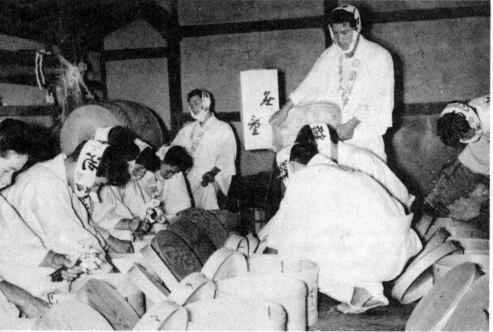

high. Each box contains a little over seven quarts of the cooked
rice. They press salt into the top of the rice in each box and then
put five small *go-hei* on top. These *go-hei* are small strips of paper
attached to a stick, a very ancient way of making offerings to the
kami. (Before the manufacture of paper, cloth seems to have been
attached to the sticks.) Each box is then covered with a lid. The
number of boxes offered each year is determined by the number
of worshippers who, having some strong wish or need, can afford the five thousand yen (about $14) which each offering box
costs. Farming people usually offer boxes asking for good rains.
Fishing people ask for safety at sea. Many families make offerings
because of other wants or needs. Anybody wanting to make an
offering must have sent his money to the shrine office by September 10; otherwise, the offering cannot be made until the following year.

The rituals open to the public usually start at 1:00 p.m. on
each of the festival days. Each young man who is to serve in the
role of swimmer carries a rice box on his shoulder to the hall of
worship for purification, both of himself and the box of rice.
After all boxes have gone through this purification procedure, the
young men go to the east side of the pond where the old shrine
to the dragon used to be. Then a *mikoshi*, or portable shrine in
which the *kami* is supposed to ride during a Shinto festival, is
carried by eight attendants wearing white clothing to the traditional stopping-place on the east side of the pond. When it has
been properly placed there, a boat is rowed out into the middle of
the pond. In the bow is a stick from which hang fairly large
paper offerings. In the stern is a taller pole from which streamers
hang.

Now comes the time for beginning the offering of the rice-
filled boxes. The first two boxes are offered by the shrine itself.
The first is to the main *kami* of the shrine; the second is to Kōen.
Since these are considered to be the most sacred offerings, only
the eldest swimmer is allowed to handle them. Then follows the
offering of the boxes paid for by individual families or worshippers.

The young men selected from the families of parishioners start the fire for cooking the rice, by the ancient method of twirling a stick rapidly in a board which has a small hole. (Chūbu region.)

Kazari-uma. At the annual festival at Fujisaki Hachiman-gū on September 15, dozens of decorated horses make their way through the city. (Kyūshū region.)

When the first box is taken into the water, the priest and all of the people bow, first in the direction of the portable shrine standing on the east shore of the pond, then to the pond itself. The priest reads a traditional prayer, *norito*, and offers *tamagushi*, a branch of the sacred evergreen tree to which strips of white paper have been attached. This offering is made to the portable shrine as that is where the *kami* is felt to be temporarily residing.

When the young men go out into the water with the numerous boxes, after the offering of the first two, they go in a line, keeping about sixty feet apart. When each gets near the center of the pond, he twirls his box in one direction. Each is responsible for so twirling his box that the rice inside gradually becomes full of water with the result that its weight overcompensates for the lightness of the wooden container. Hence the box begins to sink down into the depths, food for the waiting dragon. If the box refuses to sink, it is assumed that the young man's preparatory disciplines and purifications have not been adequate. It usually takes about a couple of hours on each day of the festival to take care of the offering of the boxes. On the occasion of our visit, as the head priest informed us later, more than two hundred boxes were offered in the three-day period. Each day, when the offerings are about completed, the portable shrine is carried back to the hall of worship and the participants on the shore begin the slow trek to their homes.

Most of the boxes so offered return to the surface within a week's time. If a box is empty, it means that the offering has been accepted and this is a good omen for the person making the offering. In case the returned box still has rice in it, the offering has not been accepted and the omen is bad. The shrine office, prior to the festival, writes the name and address of the person purchasing the offering on the box. As the boxes return to the surface of the pond, they are retrieved, washed, and purified. A piece of straw rope to which white paper strips have been attached, called a *shimenawa*, is wound around the box and it is then sent back to the person who asked that it be offered.

We walked back to the area where the buses were waiting

and became a part of the slow, one-way traffic away from the shrine back to the towns on the Tōkaidō Line. On their way back to Fukuroi, Kikugawa and Kakegawa, the buses stopped at two near-by Buddhist temples of the Pure Land sect, one named Ren-shōji and the other Saidenji. Many of the women on our bus had been discussing the rising prices of candles and incense used at these temples in the offerings made to Kōen and Hōnen. In spite of the price increases which they were grumbling about, many of the women got off in order to conclude properly the religious activities of the day. The rest of us returned to Fukuroi, some to stay overnight in a Japanese inn before making the return trip to our various homes.

This popular annual festival at the Shinto shrine of Sakura-ga-ike thus draws upon folk traditions, Buddhist legends, and ancient Shinto practices in a fashion rather typical of the Japanese religious scene. Though the interpretations of these rituals have varied from period to period, the rituals themselves have remained essentially the same. What is the force that attracts Japanese in such large numbers to special shrine festivals of this sort—festivals, incidentally, that have never had any connection with the "national" rituals which the Japanese government made compulsory at many shrines in the end of the nineteenth century in its effort to unify the nation through government-supported "national" Shinto?

In the case of the shrine at Sakura-ga-ike it is definitely not the result of any pressure or advertising on the part of the family which has had the priestly role here for centuries. The present head priest, who inherited his position, just like dozens of others, by the simple fact of being born into a given family, has tried to resign his position. The people in the district will not allow him to do so. They pay him a small monthly salary to keep him attached to the shrine, though his interests lie elsewhere in a small town where he operates a business of his own. He returns to the shrine normally only for the festival days.

Is it the desire of the individual for good luck or prosperity that brings many persons long distances? Charms and talismans are purchased by the visitors for a small price at the shrine. But these people could go to any number of shrines nearer their own homes for their good-luck charms. Is it, perhaps, that many of these people feel some sense of identification with the "way of the *kami*" of the centuries past, and this is one way they express their identification with it? These are some of the questions that rise in the mind of the person who wishes to try to understand the part played by the ancient tradition of Shinto in the life of modern Japan.

CHAPTER TWO

The Japanese Myth

MYTH AND THE SEARCH FOR MEANING

The myths and rituals of the Sakura-ga-ike Shrine, described in the preceding chapter, seem to relate more to the needs or desires of families than to a whole nation or people. However, there are some myths which primarily relate to a whole people as such, rather than to the needs of fishermen, say, or of rice cultivators. To understand a people, it is necessary to understand the basic myth through which they see themselves, their place in history, their destiny. A vital myth lives below the level of full consciousness, adding a certain tone or nuance to much of what happens in the life of the group and of the individuals who share in it. Myth has been and still is one of the ways in which man who knows so little, but who aspires to know so much, tries to find meaning in his experience and some supporting purpose in nature or his universe. Myth-making can be well described as a by-product of man's search for orientation and direction. Myths should never have been dismissed as merely pre-scientific efforts on the part of "primitive peoples" to explain beginnings. A tribe or a culture's self-image is reflected to a significant degree in the myths it clings to or transmits from generation to generation.

At a certain stage in the history of a people, its myths are "rationalized" or "organized" and edited. That is, they are converted into doctrines or dogmas and are taught self-consciously as things to be "believed." This is the process known as indoctrination, and modern secular cultures engage in it fully as much as earlier religious cultures which have reached a certain stage of self-consciousness. This process takes place through the agency either of the priest-theologian or of the ruler-politician. (In very early societies, these roles were combined.) For one major section of Christendom, the Christian myth of the role of the redeeming Son of God found a philosophical culmination in the work of Thomas Aquinas, an interpretation which was later declared to be definitive by Roman Catholic authority. The apostle Paul's interpretation of the same mythic theme was to form the basis for most of the Protestant reformers' interpretations which were then taught as doctrines to be believed. In the case of Japan, at least two thousand years ago the Yamato clan seems to have asserted the priority of its myth over the myths of the clans which it subjugated. Thus the divine ancestress of the Yamato clan gradually came to be accepted as the divine ancestress of all the Japanese people.

In all such cases, a non-mythic factor is introduced into mythic themes and the myth begins to be used as a means of social conformity or control on the part of those in positions of leadership. Such ecclesiastical and political use of myth can be dangerous in the long run. When myths are used to defend specific historical institutions or specific interpretations of the "will of God," not only do they tend to make absolute for the credulous what ought to be regarded as quite relative, but the myths also lose something of their original vitality as expressions of the subconscious and as sources of orientation and creative insight for individuals. Instead, they become instruments of political control or of tribal expansion, bringing grief to those who stand in their "divinely" self-appointed way. When the Israelites under Joshua crossed over into the region west of the Jordan River in Palestine, under the command to exterminate the people there, they did so in terms of a specific interpretation of the "will of Yahweh," their god.

Myths do influence the course of history, and rather dramatically so in the case of "rationalized" myths. In modern times the Marxist myth of the "classless society" and the "withering

away of the state" has profoundly shaped the history of the twentieth century, but there is no evidence to date that such a condition will ever occur. Similarly, since the first century of our era,
many Christians have believed in the "second coming" of the
Christ, and this has influenced their attitude toward life and their
practical behavior in many respects, though the "second coming"
seems as non-realizable as the "withering away of the state."

The fact that people can be made to "believe" in myths that
are self-consciously promoted, is a potent factor not to be forgotten. Rarely do we ourselves live by the rational standards we
expect others to abide by. People believe and act because of some
prior, non-rational disposition to believe and act. That prior disposition is not unrelated to man's need for meaningful relatedness.
For centuries European-Western man has lived with the mythic
conviction that there is a "Purpose" in history, or a goal or end.
He has believed there is a "Power" in control of the process or
working immanently through it. For the Christian this "Power"
has usually been thought of as "Personal." For the Marxist, it is
non-personal but just as potent. Such mythic convictions as these
are far from dead in the West. When we turn to Japan, we find
a different type of myth. Let us present that myth briefly, and
then turn to some problems of its interpretation.

THE BASIC JAPANESE MYTH[1]

Out of the primordial chaos, which was like an ocean of
mud veiled in darkness, three *kami* sprang. The head of this triad
was Master of the Center of Heaven. The other two were High
Producing Kami and Divine Producing Kami.* There is a reference
to the chief *kami* standing motionless in the center of the cosmos.
These three *kami* were born without progenitors and hid them-

---

* I have taken the liberty of abbreviating the titles in the English translations instead of
following B. H. Chamberlain (*Kojiki or Records of Ancient Matters*) in his more literal
renderings. In only a few cases have I felt it desirable to retain the Japanese name, usually in a shortened form.

selves without leaving any posterity.[2] Other *kami* sprang out of
the primeval chaos spontaneously and independently of each
other and they became invisible. Finally there appear Izanagi-
no-kami, the Male Who Invites, and Izanami-no-kami, the Female Who Invites. The heavenly *kami* order these two to make,
consolidate, and give birth to the drifting land. They are given a
spear and, standing on the floating bridge of heaven, they push
the spear down into the mist, searching for land as they stir the
briny silt below. As they draw up the spear, the brine from its
tip forms the Island of Onogoro.

Descending to this island, Izanagi and Izanami see to the
erection of a pillar and a palace. Examining their bodies closely
they notice their sexual differences and desire for sexual union
comes upon them. Going around the pillar, one to the right and
the other to the left, they meet on the far side. Izanami speaks
first saying, "Oh, what a beautiful and amiable youth." Izanagi
replies, "Oh, what a beautiful and amiable maiden." Then they
embrace as man and wife. From their first union is born Hiruko,
"child of the sun." The child is not regarded as good and is put
into a boat and set adrift. The next child is also repudiated. Thereupon Izanagi and Izanami return to heaven to find out why their
first offspring have not been good ones.

A divination is then held in heaven. As a result of this, the
divine pair are told that the fault lay in the female's having
spoken first. "Descend back again and amend your words." There
immediately follows an account of the birth of the eight great
islands and then the smaller islands. After giving birth to all the
countries, they give birth to more *kami*.[3] In all, Izanagi and Izanami procreate eighty countries, eight hundred myriads of *kami*,
the Great Eight Island Land (an ancient name for Japan), the
sea, mountains, rivers, and so on. The last *kami* born from the pair
is the Fire Kami. Izanami is burnt so badly in giving birth to him
that she dies and withdraws to the underworld.

This, in outline, is the first portion of the myth. Before proceeding to the second part, which became an important element in
later Japanese history because of its political implications, let us
look at a few contrasts between this myth and the familiar bibli-

cal myth so that we can see some of the real differences between the Japanese and the Near Eastern and Western ways of taking hold of life.

SOME INTERESTING CONTRASTS

Strictly speaking, the Japanese myth is not a creation myth. Izanagi and Izanami are not *kami* of creation but *kami* of pro-creation and production. All the *kami* who precede them symbolize the process of becomingness or evolution, quite possibly. The ancient Japanese had practically no interest in the idea of creation. Chinese influence on Japanese writers goes far to explain the first abstract *kami* mentioned in the narrative. It is Izanagi and Izanami who are the important *kami*. All things that come into being after their arrival on the scene are procreated sexually or appear spontaneously. The symbolism is quite concrete; there is nothing abstract here. It should be noted also that everything which was produced was called *kami* without exception, even the mountains, the lakes, and the sea.

This entire picture is in rather sharp contrast with the Judeo-Christian myth based upon the early chapters of Genesis and elaborated in detail by theologians of many schools in later centuries. In the biblical myth, the world is created by divine fiat or command. God said, "Let there be light!" and there was light. As some of the schoolmen were to phrase it, God created out of nothing. This God is a transcendent being. This idea of a transcendent God became an important element in the western concept of dualism—a dualism between God and Satan, supernature and nature, good and evil, spirit and flesh.

In the Shinto myth, all the stress is on immanence and the continuity between procreators and procreated. Everything is divine, *kami*-like. All things proceed from heavenly divine spirit. The Shinto myth and its later interpreters say nothing about any "purpose" in creation. In contrast, Western thought says a great deal about "God's purpose" in creating. Moreover, in the Genesis account man is set over against nature, man is turned against woman and woman is turned against man, and man is turned against God because he has violated a command of God. In the Shinto myth there is no hint of opposition or estrangement. Thus in Shinto there has never been any necessity to try to "justify the ways of God to men." No Milton's *Paradise Lost* could appear. As G. B. Sansom has said, "Oriental literature in general freely discusses man's duties but not his claims or his rights. I do not think it occurs to most Oriental philosophers to question the universe. It is examined, and perhaps found wanting by some of them; but they do not generally feel impelled to seek justification for its shortcomings."[4]

The absence of the ideas of a transcendent deity in Shinto who creates man with "free will" and then severely punishes him for using it, explains many of the differences in mood between it and orthodox Christianity. The word *musubi* which occurs in the name of two of the initial triad of *kami*, comes from *musubu*, which means to grow, to tie, to bind. This involves the idea of a power immanent in nature; in other words, creative evolution.

Another contrast between the biblical myth and the Shinto myth is the absence from the Genesis account of anything resembling the role and figure of Izanami, the female *kami*. What symbols of the feminine were present in the ancient Semitic myth before the Yahwist priests or scribes edited the narrative, we do not know. But Shinto thought has always allowed full equality to the female principle along with the male. Only later did the Japanese patriarchy make slight emendations in the tradition, probably reflected in the heavenly *kamis'* instructions to Izanami, after their initial failure, that the male *kami* should speak first. This would seem to reflect a fundamentally different attitude toward femininity and probably also toward sexuality in the two traditions.

The spear granted to Izanagi and Izanami has been interpreted as being the male phallus or Chinese "jewel stalk." Hirata Atsutane, one of the great scholars of the Shinto renaissance, conjectured that this spear was *o-bashira*, male pillar.[5] More probably it refers to *tree* as a pillar. From ancient times the tree was a very common symbol of the presence of *kami*. A more abstract interpretation of the spear has also been made, that it was the earth-axis which appears in many other mythologies. When Izanagi and Izanami drew up the spear, the drippings from its point formed an island. On this island they erected the august pillar and a palace.* Then they proceeded to become more intimately acquainted with each other. Chamberlain's translation lapses into Latin at this point, but Aston's translation of the *Nihonshoki*, appearing fourteen years later, puts the account into rather general English. The necessity for such a circumlocution would never have occurred to a Shinto scholar. The dialogue between the two *kami* as given by Aston in the *Nihongi* is as follows:

> Then Izanagi inquired of the female deity, saying: "In thy body is there aught formed?" She answered and said: "In my body there is a place which is the source of femininity." The male deity said: "In my body again there is a place which is the source of masculinity, I wish to unite this source-place of my body to the source-place of thy body." Hereupon the male and female first became united as husband and wife.[6]

Nowhere in the Shinto tradition is the sex act associated with morbidity or guilt feelings. It is as normal as the eating of food and is the central symbol of growth and creation.

The first child born of the union of Izanagi and Izanami was Hiruko, Sun Male Child.[7] Why this *kami* did not play an important part in the written mythology we cannot definitely say. There is an interpretation accepted by some Japanese scholars that Hiruko was the *kami* worshipped by early solar-worshipping tribes who had male priests, but these were overwhelmed at some time by a group who had a cult of solar worship presided over by female priests.

---

* On Awaji Island in the Inland Sea is a great tumulus which popular legend declares was once an island. It is named Onogoro and on it is a shrine dedicated to Izanagi and Izanami. As to the heavenly bridge on which the pair stood when they dipped the spear down into the mists below them, Motoori Norinaga (1730-1801) claimed it was a real bridge, and he found traces of it and bridges like it at several points along the Japanese coast. Motoori had a tendency to interpret the narratives literally. In some interpretations of the myth, the bridge came to be interpreted as the rainbow.

The account of the divination held in heaven to discover why Hiruko and the following child were subject to defects, tells us something interesting about the Japanese way of thinking of *kami*. The heavenly *kami* obviously did not know the reason for the failure or they would not have resorted to divination. In other words, omniscience is a concept quite foreign to Shinto ways of thinking. So is omnipotence. No *kami* sees all, knows all, or predestines all. Shinto can come to terms with theories of pragmatism and of relativism, but it cannot deal with philosophical notions of an Absolute or with the notion of a predestinating God.

A brief comment is called for concerning the mythic account of the birth of the Fire Kami or Fire Generating Kami, as a result of whose birth Izanami dies. D. C. Holtom, following a hint provided by E. M. Satow, interprets this naturalistically. He sees the *kami* as standing for early man's experience of an earth that was parched, dried, and glittering in an intense heat. He feels this reflects something out of the early environment of some portion of the Japanese people before they migrated to the islands of Japan.[8] Such an interpretation is, of course, possible. But in the light of some of the more modern work in comparative mythology, it is just as possible that this is a reflection in the ancient Japanese myth of the emergence of consciousness. In many mythologies fire and light are very definitely symbols of awareness, awakening, or spiritual illumination. With the birth of conscious awareness, the primal unity of the instinctive life is broken. Man becomes aware of his finitude; he senses separation. He knows the fear of death. The birth of consciousness is the death of "innocence" or unconscious union with the Great Mother. The Great Mother then withdraws to some distance. This brings us to the next chapter in the myth narrative.

THE BASIC SHINTO MYTH CONTINUED

Izanami, being badly burnt at the birth of the Fire Kami, becomes very sick. Various *kami* are born from the products of her body before she "divinely retires" to the underworld, the world of the dead. Izanagi, in wrath, draws his sword and proceeds to cut the Fire Kami into pieces. In this process many other *kami* are born. Then Izanagi decides to go to the underworld to see his wife. He finds her dwelling place and talks with her, asking her to return to the upper world again. She pleads with him to wait but not to look upon her. In his impatience, contrary to her request, he lights the end pieces from his comb and looks upon her, only to see a hideous sight. Thereupon he flees, pursued by the ugly forces of the underworld and finally by Izanami herself. He throws behind him various possessions as he flees, to hold off his pursuers; and he finally reaches the upper world where he has to purify himself from his journey.

What interpretation should be made of the slaying of the Fire Kami? Holtom describes it as a picture-poem depicting a terrific thunderstorm. The sword of the sky-father, Izanagi, is the lightning flash. Behind the myth Holtom sees the universal human experience of wonder and awe when man stands in the presence of a tremendous storm. At the hilt of the sword there are dark rain, dark swift water, and mountain-like clouds; on the blade, fire and thunder; at the point, the splintering of trees and rocks.[9]

However, a psychological interpretation, similar to the one made above regarding the birth of the Fire Kami, is just as probable, especially if we bear in mind the ancient mythic traditions of India. With the birth of consciousness comes a separation which is often reflected in widely separated myths as a slaying or a dismemberment of some cosmic creature, whether the "Cosmic Man" (Purusha) of the ancient Hindu tradition, or the dragon slain by the dragon slayer, or "the lamb slain from the foundation of the world" (as reflected in a portion of the Semitic myth). In other mythic traditions, as in the Maori creation myth, it is the World Parents who are separated rather than slain. All these accounts reflect the feeling or intuition that there is a creating that goes on in nature prior to the emergence of consciousness, and a creating that goes on after the birth of consciousness. Izanagi, the sky-father and male principle (universal symbol of consciousness in the mythology of the human race), creates by cutting up and sundering. The creative process, begun by the primal pair together, now continues but not in the same way as when the male principle stood in full and intimate relationship with the female principle.

In the Japanese myth, Izanami does not seem to fulfill one of the important requirements of the Great Mother Goddess of all early religions, the source of fertility. For, having withdrawn to the underworld, Izanami apparently does not make an annual return in the spring. However, it is quite possible that in the prehistoric period of Japan, Izanami may well have been the Earth Mother who annually withdrew from the world, to return again in the spring with the returning vegetation. Holtom cites a ritual used in the fire-subduing ceremony which is probably very ancient. In this ritual the events of Izanami's death and her journey to the lower world are recounted, and the narrative continues:

> When she reached the even hill of Yomi she thought and said, "In the upper world, ruled over by my beloved husband, I have begotten and left behind a child of evil heart." So, returning, she yet again gave birth to children, to the Deity of Water, Gourd, River Leaves, and Clay Mountain Lady—to these four kinds of things she gave birth. Then she taught Izanagi, saying, "Whenever the heart of this evil-hearted child becomes violent, subdue it with the Deity of Water, with Gourd, with Clay Mountain Lady, and with River Leaves."[10]

That this Earth Mother function of Izanami never became a permanent part of the main stream of the Japanese myth may well be traceable to the political use made of another portion of the myth. In any event, it is quite possible that Izanami originally was the Great Mother Goddess as found in other mythologies. There is no contradiction between her being both Mother Earth, the source of life and vegetation, and the symbol of death. The earth is both womb and tomb.

Having become polluted by his visit to the underworld, Izanagi proceeds to purify himself at a river-mouth. Various *kami* are born in the process of his purification, but the one of most importance in later Japanese history is Amaterasu-Ōmi-kami, the Heavenly Shining One. She is born from his left eye. From his right eye is born Tsuki-yomi-no-kami, Moon Kami, while from his nose is born Susanoo-no-mikoto, Brave Swift Impetuous Male, often known simply as the Storm God. Traditions differ as to whether Amaterasu-Ōmikami was born from Izanagi alone or from the divine pair, Izanagi and Izanami.* To Amaterasu was given the Plain of High Heaven to rule. Tsuki-yomi-no-kami was given the realm of night to rule, and Susanoo was sent down to rule the earth.[11] Since Amaterasu became of central importance in the later history of Japan, it is necessary that we deal with her place in the myth in some detail.

The Moon Kami is not referred to again in the *Kojiki,* and both the *Kojiki* and the *Nihonshoki* devote a great deal of space to the activities of Susanoo, who proved to be less than a harmonious ruler. In view of the known rivalry which existed historically in early Japan between the clan or clans situated in Izumo, on the west coast, and the Yamato clan, which seems to have started its conquest of the islands from Kyushu in the south, in this myth cycle we probably get more than hints of actual occurrences. Without going into the details and their many variants in the *Nihonshoki,* let us look at the cycle of stories briefly.

Susanoo, instead of taking up his duties properly, becomes quite violent and causes damage to mountains and rivers. Thereupon Izanagi orders him to descend to the underworld to rule there. Susanoo replies that first he wants to visit his sister Amaterasu. Amaterasu takes alarm and confronts him in a militant posture, wanting to know his intentions. To prove that his intentions are good, Susanoo persuades Amaterasu to swear an oath with him and mutually produce children. Amaterasu produces her children by chewing up Susanoo's sword, and he produces his children by chewing up her string of curved jewels. According to the account in the *Kojiki,* Susanoo draws the conclusion

---

* M. Anesaki, *History of Japanese Religion,* Kegan Paul, Trench, Trubner, London, 1930, p. 25, note 1, held that the male-alone theory was the later version.

that he has proved his peaceful intentions, but he immediately proceeds to break down the divisions of the heavenly rice fields, fill up the ditches, and pollute with excrement the hall in which Amaterasu performs the annual festival of first-fruits. His violence finally reaches the point where he breaks through the roof of her weaving hall, and lets fall into it a horse which he has flayed backwards.* As a result of these actions, Amaterasu withdraws into a rock cave and shuts the door tightly.

A heavenly council is called to deal with Susanoo. It is decided to expel him from heaven. So Susanoo descends to the land of Izumo. The *Kojiki* then includes a whole cycle of stories centering around Susanoo and his descendants, in the area around Izumo on the main island of Japan. Reports come back to heaven that the place is "painfully unproarious." Various messengers are sent down to pacify the land, but they are unable to resist the temptation of staying in Izumo, and thus no report ever gets back to heaven. Finally a compromise is worked out with Great Land Master Kami (Ō-Kuninushi-no-kami), a descendant of Susanoo, and his sons. Izumo consents to accept the rule of a heaven-descended grandson if a high palace or temple is built for the Izumo *kami*.

The stories in the *Nihonshoki* lean in the direction of the Izumo clan, and the stories in the *Kojiki* reflect the perspective of the Yamato clan. Back of the language of the myths is an actual historical conflict between two opposing groups. The "heavenly messengers" were very possibly envoys sent out by the Yamato clan in Kyushu to sound out the Izumo clan on some division of rule.[12] Evidently there were serious problems involved in the early contacts between the conquerors coming up from Kyushu in the south, worshipping a *kami* called Amaterasu, and the people dwelling around Izumo, on the western shores of Honshu. The *Kami* of Izumo were associated with the underworld and thus were regarded as agents of the realm of mystery. But Great Land Master Kami worked for the welfare of the people in his domain, aided by a *kami* associated with the power of healing. Traditionally the *kami* of Izumo have been worshipped when there have

---

* To flay an animal backwards alive was considered a mark of cruelty in Japan.

Tsushima Jinja. Enshrines Susanoo-no-mikoto, a *kami* providing relief from pestilence and danger. (Chūbu region.)

Miyazaki Jingū. A shrine dedicated to the first Emperor, Jimmu. (Kyūshū region.)

been pestilences, or in times of disaster.[13] It is this Great Land Master Kami which is worshipped as the main *kami* at Izumo Shrine, one of the very old Shinto shrines in Japan.

After the agreement is made with Izumo, Amaterasu commissions her grandson to descend and rule. To him, Ninigi-no-mikoto, she says: "The Luxuriant Land of Reed Plains is a country which our descendants are to inherit. Go, therefore, Our Imperial Grandson, and rule over it! And may Our Imperial lineage continue unbroken and prosperous, co-eternal with Heaven and Earth!"[14] After the descent of the heavenly grandchild, the records describe quite a series of adventures. Then the Divine Ages come to an end. Myth allegedly gives way to history. The first human emperor appears, Jimmu Tennō.[15]

According to the pre-war official chronology, Jimmu Tennō was born in 711 B.C. and acceded to the throne in 660 B.C. Jimmu is the name which was conferred on him many centuries after his death. According to the *Kojiki*, Jimmu was the direct descendant of the Sun Goddess, Amaterasu, through her grandson, Ninigi-no-mikoto.[16] The thousand years of history from Jimmu Tennō down to about 400 A.D. must be regarded as purely legendary, but these legends have played an important part in the history of Japan from time to time. Jimmu's conquests of rebellious tribes began in Kyushu. Gradually he extended his domains onto the main island of Honshu. The *Nihonshoki* quotes him as saying: "I have heard that in the East there is a fair land encircled on all sides by blue mountains. . . . I think that this land will undoubtedly be suitable for the extension of the Heavenly task, so that its glory should fill the universe. It is, doubtless, the center of the world." Aston says of this speech that it is entirely Chinese in every respect, "and it is preposterous to put it in the mouth of an Emperor who is supposed to have lived more than a thousand years before the introduction of Chinese learning into Japan."[17]

According to the *Nihonshoki*, before Jimmu Tennō was able to establish his capital in these delightful eastern lands, he spent six years in subduing the tribes. Finally taking possession of the

Kansai area (center of modern Osaka and Kyoto), he established his capital at Kashiwabara. There he deposited the Three Sacred Treasures, the mirror, the sword, and the jewels, which had been given by Amaterasu to Ninigi-no-mikoto. On the occasion of his accession to the throne, Jimmu Tennō is supposed to have uttered the words: "In regard to matters that are above, We shall respond to the goodness of the Heavenly Powers in granting us the Kingdom. And in regard to matters that are below, We shall foster righteousness and extend the line of the imperial descendants. Thereafter, the capital shall be extended so as to embrace all the six cardinal points, and the eight cords may be covered so as to form a roof. Will this not be well?"[18]

Where the ancient Japanese acquired their idea of the divine descent of their ruler is still a matter of debate. Some say it was brought from Southeast Asia by the people who invaded ancient Japan. F. J. Horner points out that the tradition of divine kingship was widespread throughout Southeast Asia and the islands of the Pacific. A claim to divine sovereignty by a particular ruler, for example the Yamato chieftain, would be much more readily accepted by people who had been brought up to believe in the divine origin of kings. It is also possible that in ancient times there was a female sovereign whose political career was connected with a solar myth. According to an old Chinese history, there was a country to the east of China ruled by a queen without a husband.[19] Griffis says of the conquest by the Yamato clan: "By the might not only of superior weapons but of intellect the Yamato men wrought progress, conquering by Shinto, that is, theology, as well as with iron. Seen through official spectacles, the conquerors' ancestors came from 'Heaven.' They were a divine race sprung from the 'gods,' while those subdued were earthborn and therefore ordained to subjection."[20]

The myth of solar phenomena, whatever its origin, Chinese, Korean, or Japanese, was fused with political interests. A dogma regarding earthly rulers was grafted onto an older body of material. Conqueror and conquered seem to have tried to adapt their myths to some degree to take this into account. It is certain that both the *Kojiki* and the *Nihonshoki* were compiled in the interests of fortifying dynastic claims in the presence of rival political interests in the seventh and eighth centuries.[21]

Hence, from before the time of the written documents, the *Kojiki* and the *Nihonshoki*, two elements already mingled in the narratives regarding Amaterasu. There was the mythic side and there was the political side. As a myth, the stories about Amaterasu probably represent the beliefs of an agricultural people in the life-giving power of the sun. Somewhere along the line, Amaterasu was associated with a male counterpart, Taka-mi-musubi-no-kami, "High-Producing Deity" (as translated by Anesaki). Taka-mi-musubi-no-kami seems to have been always associated with Amaterasu as a hidden or higher entity, emphasizing growth. Also near her is a female associate, Toyo-uke-no-kami, "Abundance Bounty Deity," a goddess of food.* Her origin is disputed. In the reign of the twenty-first emperor, Yūryaku, the shrine of this *kami* of food was moved from Tamba to Ise. Her shrine there is known as the Gekū or Outer Shrine.

Many scholars lean toward the conclusion that a myth of the sun is the proper key to an understanding of the original nature of Amaterasu.** Historically, except for short periods, this has been overshadowed by the stress put on her role as divine ancestress of the chiefs of the early Yamato clan. As the Yamato clan extended its sway from Kyushu up to the area around Nara, the legends and myths of the Yamato people gained increasing sway over the minds of the people who were subjugated. By the third or fourth century A.D., the Yamato rulers were not only political sovereigns but also chief priests of a religion which centered primarily in Amaterasu. They claimed direct descent from her, and as a by-product of this belief in the divine origin of the ruling house, gradually there developed the concept of the divine origin of the Japanese people.

---

* Also called Ō-Getsu-hime-no-kami.
** Needless to say, during the period of militant nationalism in Japan in the 1930's, Japanese scholars were not inclined to go into such questions publicly.

CHAPTER THREE

Shinto Ideas of *Kami*

What can a modern person, oriented toward the use of scientific tools of inquiry and with an agnostic attitude toward all concepts of the divine, do when confronted with stories about the doings of the gods? Many persons seem to solve the problem by taking an attitude of disbelief toward all such stories. Others solve it by believing only the stories from their own tradition. However, in my estimation there is another approach which is far more profitable. This approach studies the phenomena sympathetically on the assumption that ideas about, and practices pertaining to, the mythic and divine realm can tell us a great deal about the human beings involved. To be sympathetic does not mean to be uncritical. This approach also involves acceptance of the working hypothesis that man's ideas of the gods can tell us something about *man*, without involving the seeker in the theological question as to what it may tell us about *more-than-man*.

THE MEANING OF *KAMI*

The key word for the divine in Shinto is *kami*. When Chamberlain published his English translation of the *Kojiki*, near the end of the nineteenth century, he used the word "deity" for *kami*. In his introduction he wrote, "Of all the words for which it is hard to find a suitable English equivalent, *Kami* is the hardest. Indeed there is no English word which renders it with any near approach to exactness. If therefore it is here rendered by the word

'deity' ('deity' being preferred to 'god' because it includes superior beings of both sexes), it must be clearly understood that
the word 'deity' is taken in a sense not sanctioned by any English
dictionary. . . ."[1] Many Westerners followed Chamberlain in his
effort to translate the term, some using the word "god." Even some
Japanese scholars fell into the practice.

Various explanations of the term *kami* have been offered.
The one still most commonly heard (and Chamberlain gave cre-
dence to it in his introduction to the *Kojiki*) is that *kami* means
"above," "upper," or "superior." This interpretation goes back
to Arai Hakuseki (1657-1725), but the famous scholar of the
Shinto renaissance, Motoori Norinaga (1730-1801), pointed out
that this idea was mistaken. Modern Japanese scholars in philol-
ogy, following Motoori's theory, point out that in the Nara period (710-794) there were several terms for *kami* and their pro-
nunciations differed. Nowadays it is admitted that the etymologi-
cal method is fruitless in arriving at the meaning of the term
kami.

Another explanation of the word *kami* comes from the Kamakura period. According to this interpretation, *kami* came from
the word for mirror, *kagami*. A later interpretation connects the
word *kami* with *kakurimi*, from *kakureru*, to become invisible.[2]
While it is generally true according to Shinto that *kami* are not
visible, there are some *kami* that can be seen, and in Folk Shinto
the object itself is treated as the *kami*.

When Western writers use the words "god," "deity," or
"God" for *kami*, they are confusing Western ways of thinking
with Japanese ways of feeling. We do well to remember that in
Shinto *kami* stands for that which is "divine" in some sense of
the term but not in a specific Western sense. It stands for that
which is everywhere present in varying degrees, and it stands for
that which is not entirely present or visible to people. It stands for
mystery, for the feeling of "awesomeness" akin to the sense of
"the holy" as described by some writers. If *kami* is to be understood in its fuller Shinto sense, it must be experienced in the context which lies beyond words or theological concepts. In the context of the living Shinto tradition, *kami* is something to be re-

spected. *Kami* provides the power for all growth, for development and creativity. *Kami* is something to make man "walk on," to progress toward his hopes. *Kami* is in nature and man is in nature also, and *kami* is in man. Faith in Shinto refers to the relationship between *kami* and the group and the members of the group.

SOME TYPES OF *KAMI*

The *kami* in Shinto are numerous and Japanese scholars have sought to classify them in a wide variety of ways. Our concern is not with classification but rather with showing some of the diversity of types. First might be noted the more abstract type of *kami*. In the beginning, according to the *Kojiki* account, three *kami* appeared out of the primordial chaos, as mentioned in Chapter Two. These have been evaluated differently by the scholars. Ame-no-minaka-nushi-no-kami (the *Kami*-Who-Stands-in-the-Center-of-Heaven), has sometimes been interpreted as an expression of primitive monotheism. However, Shinto itself has never shown any marked tendencies toward monotheism. It is possible that this way of thinking is the result of borrowing from Chinese concepts of deity. This would place it as late as the fifth or sixth century. Chinese influence was very strong at the time the *Kojiki* and *Nihonshoki* were being compiled, and the cosmogony of the *Nihonshoki* was borrowed from Chinese writings. The notion that Ame-no-minaka-nushi-no-kami was central in the pantheon, in the Edo period, was emphasized by Hirata Atsutane (1776-1843), under Western influence.[3]

The other two members of the original triad, Taka-mi-musubi-no-kami (High-Producing Kami), and Kami-musubi-no-kami (Divine-Producing Kami), were interpreted by some of the earlier Japanese scholars as genuine creation deities. However, the power these *kami* had was the power of being self-born *(umareru-chikara)*, not the power to create *(musu-chikara)*.[4] In general common people do not worship deities that seem abstract. However,

in Japan there is some evidence that these *musubi-kami* were regarded as ancestral *kami* by various families down to the beginning of the Heian period (the ninth century).[5]

In the preceding chapter it was indicated why the life-pro-
ducing *kami,* Izanagi and Izanami, should not be considered creation *kami.* Many *kami* were born to these two, and a number of
them have been claimed as ancestors by many famous Japanese
families. Such claims have played an important part in the system of classes, or ranks, in Japan.

Of the numerous *kami* born to Izanagi and Izanami, the one
having the highest position is Amaterasu, known in the West as
the Sun Goddess. Historically, she has been most important as the
divine ancestress of the imperial house of Yamato and, eventually,
of all the Japanese nation. This raises the question of the part
that ancestor worship played in ancient times in Japan. There
are many Japanese scholars who claim that ancient Shinto included ancestor worship as well as nature worship. Others claim
that ancestor worship was quite weak until Chinese influence
made itself felt. Kato claims that ancestor worship must have been
a part of the life of the people at the time of Jimmu Tennō, the
first emperor (660 B.C.), because according to tradition, the ancestor of the Imbe family, Ame-no-tomi-no-mikoto, built a shrine
for the purpose of worshipping his ancestral *kami.*[6]

In any event, so far as Amaterasu is concerned, she must
have been both a solar *kami* and ancestress of the ruling house of
Yamato. The solar aspects receded at an early date and her ancestral function became increasingly important. The view which
was to stress the cosmic significance of Amaterasu as Sun Goddess
developed in accordance with the Japanese political structure. Before the Edo (i.e., Tokugawa) period, it did not become a significant part of the feeling of the Japanese people in general. When
Amaterasu was moved into the central position, with the stress
on this renewed at various periods, it was not because of a theo-
retical interest in monotheism. It was because she was the ancestress of the imperial house. For example, near the beginning of
the ninth century, Imbe-no-Hironari, the author of the *Kogoshūi,*
wrote: "Now since Amaterasu-Ō-mi-kami is the greatest Ances-

tral Goddess, no other Shinto deities can claim equality, just as a son is ever inferior to his father, or a vassal to his lord.'"[7] Perhaps by the sixth or seventh century the centrality of Amaterasu had been accepted by most of the people, and there was a national shrine to her at Ise.

Susanoo, Impetuous Male, her brother, also has a prominent role in many of the stories which center in Izumo. He and his descendants ruled the country thereabouts. When the compromise was worked out with Amaterasu regarding ruling powers, Susanoo's descendants were given charge of the invisible world. The great shrine at Izumo, one of the oldest in Japan, is dedicated to his offspring, Ō-Kuni-nushi-no-kami, Great Land Master Kami.[8]

KAMI OF FOOD AND OF AGRICULTURAL PRODUCTION

It was many centuries ago that Japan emerged from a purely hunting and fishing culture into a rice-planting culture. The *kami* of rice and of food generally came to play an important part in the life of the common people. These *kami* were in no sense abstract; they presided over the mysteries of the growth process in the fields so indispensable to the life of the peasants and villagers. The cult of Inari, which has been so popular in Japan for centuries, centers in a *kami* of food, Uga-no-mikoto. (Inari shrines are dedicated to other *kami* also.) The fox is the messenger of the *kami* of food, and he usually stands guard near the entrance to the Inari shrine, or beside the main shrine.

In the very early period probably none of the *kami* were thought of as being as strong as the forces of nature. But when the Japanese people settled down and became agriculturalists, some of the *kami* gradually came to be thought of as controlling nature for the benefit of the people's food supply. At Hirose Shrine, for example, the *kami* of food was often petitioned to work for the welfare of crops, and at Tatsuta Shrine, not too far distant, the *kami* of rain was appealed to for assistance.

Whether or not ancestor worship was a prominent feature of the life of the early Japanese people before Chinese influence became pronounced, is still debated by the scholars. But at a fairly early date Amaterasu became the most important ancestral *kami* because she was the ancestress of the imperial house. According to the earliest written records, there were other families who claimed a *kami* as their ancestor. For example, the Nakatomi from whom the Fujiwara family later emerged claimed as their guardian *kami* and as their ancestor Ame-no-koyane-no-mikoto.* Apparently it gradually became the custom for the high-ranking families to claim *kami* as ancestors.

By the fifth century the whole system of ranks or classes had become quite confused, with many families claiming connection with noble families to which they had no real right. To belong to a noble family meant more worldly benefits as well as a higher-ranking *kami* as ancestor. Thus the nineteenth emperor, Ingyō (412-453), ordered the rectification of falsities in family histories. The decree which he issued refers to families who described themselves as descendants of emperors, or attributed to their group a miraculous origin, saying their ancestors came down from heaven. The houses had multiplied to the point where there were 10,000 surnames of doubtful authenticity. Hence he ordered the performance of *kugadachi*—the putting of one's hand into boiling water. "Let the people of the various Houses and surnames wash themselves and practice abstinence, and let them, each one calling the gods to witness, plunge their hands in boiling water." Everyone involved was told to go to a particular spur of Amagashi Hill, with the admonition that "He who tells the truth will be uninjured; he who is false will assuredly suffer harm." The *Nihonshoki* records that many who had falsified their titles, watching others get their hands burnt in the boiling water, slipped quietly away.[9]

The *kami* of the clan or kinship group (called *uji-gami*) are the *kami* which have been perhaps the most important *kami* of all during the long period of Shinto history, at least up to modern times. These *kami* of the clans seem originally to have been associ-

---

* Originally enshrined at Hiraoka, it was later enshrined at Kasuga in Nara.

ated with specific people or clans, rather than with specific places. Up to the end of the Heian period the function of the *uji-gami* was to protect the *uji*, the kinship group. However, during the Kamakura period (twelfth to fourteenth centuries) the Japanese landowner system was changed and the clan system collapsed. Thus the meaning of the term *uji-gami* gradually changed. It came to stand not only for the tutelary deity of kinship groups, but also for the tutelary deity of a specific place or section of land. There are several theories regarding these guardian *kami*. One of the more commonly held theories is that these *kami* were associated with the place where one was born and lived. They were guardians of a specific place. When a family moved into a new district, it began to worship the guardian *kami* of the new place. In modern times the two terms, *uji-gami* and *kami* of the place *(chinju-no kami; ubusunagami)*, have become intermingled. As the Japanese have moved increasingly into the big cities, the *uji-gami* system has broken down further.

SO-CALLED "KAMI OF MORALITY"

Motoori classified the *kami* in several ways. One of these distinctions was between the *kami* excelling in goodness and the *kami* excelling in badness. The idea seems to have come from China, and was influenced by popular Taoism, among other things. Some were to follow Motoori in this idea, even appealing to the basic Shinto myth to support their interpretation. Hirata Atsutane did not follow this idea, however, and his is the more reliable interpretation. In the chapter on Shinto ethics, this will be treated in more detail in connection with the *kami* referred to in the mythical narrative. At this point it is sufficient to say that there is no ethical dualism in Shinto. When a "bad" *kami* is referred to in Shinto writings, there is no thought of *ethical* badness but rather a *kami* who is violent or troublesome. Similarly, there is no such thing as a "good" *kami* in the strictly ethical sense, though there are *kami* who specialize in making things work out for the best, making straight what has been distorted or bent.

GO-SHINTAI, OR OBJECTS OF WORSHIP

According to Shinto, no *kami* ordinarily has a form or reveals its figure. However, an important part is played by the *go-shintai,* an object of worship in which the spirit of a *kami* is believed to reside. The *go-shintai* is treated with great reverence. It is a symbol only, and is not the *kami* itself, but at festivals it is often treated as though it were the *kami* itself. At Ise Grand Shrine the sacred mirror is treated as though it were Amaterasu herself, but the mirror is not Amaterasu. At Ō-Miwa Shrine in Nara province, the mountain itself is the *go-shintai* and the common people do not trespass on the mountain.

Even after the introduction of Buddhism into Japan, Shinto was not inclined to try to express *kami* through the use of images. After the Heian period and growing out of certain philosophical developments, some Shinto shrines did allow images of the Buddha to be introduced. Not far from Kumano Shrine, up in the mountains, I climbed by a narrow path to a place of worship which had a Buddhist statue as its *go-shintai.* One of the elderly shrine believers quietly opened the door of the little sanctuary to allow me to photograph it in the dim light which filtered through the surrounding trees.

More often, polished stones, swords, bows and arrows, or mirrors are used as *go-shintai.* Whenever this object is taken out for the festival procession, the head priest handles it very carefully and screens it from view so no ordinary person may look upon the sacred object. At Kumano Hayatama Shrine, when the priest was carrying the *go-shintai* back to the main shrine after its temporary stopping at a wayside worship spot near the river, no person or car was allowed to pass the priest. This would have been regarded as very disrespectful to the symbol of the *kami.*

Sometimes *kami* are in the form of animals. The *Nihonshoki* includes a story of the emperor who wanted to see the form of the *kami* of Mount Mimoro, and he commanded one of his followers to go and seize it. The man came back with a great serpent whose eyeballs flamed. The emperor was afraid and fled into the interior of the palace.[10] *Kami* are also seen in the wolf, tiger, hare, wild white boar, white deer, and the crow.

MI-TAMA AS "SOUL OF KAMI"

The word *mi-tama* is ordinarily translated as "soul." *Mi* is an honorific and *tama* stands for *tamashii*, soul.* Apparently the ancient Japanese believed in four kinds of souls or spirits: (1) *ara-mi-tama,* rough or violent soul; (2) *nigi-mi-tama,* quiet, tranquil, or mature soul; (3) *saki-mi-tama,* luck spirit; and (4) *kushi-mi-tama,* mysterious, awesome, or wondrous spirit. Many meanings have been given to these terms but no one interpretation is fixed.

Ara-mi-tama and *nigi-mi-tama* always confront each other. In ancient times, *ara* and *nigi* were always used as pairs, for example, *ara-tae* (rough cloth) and *nigi-tae* (soft cloth). *Ara* in general carried the connotation of rough or rugged, and *nigi* meant soft or refined. *Ara-mi-tama* when applied to *kami* seems to have described the working of *kami* when the works were violent or on the rough side. *Nigi-mi-tama* referred to the actions of *kami* when the actions were gentle, matured, or harmonious.

This can be well illustrated by the stories about Empress Jingū, wife of Emperor Chūai who ruled Japan from 192–200 A.D. Jingū outlived her husband by many years and, obedient to an oracle emanating from Amaterasu, she went with her troops to Shiragi (modern Korea). She miraculously held off the birth of her child by means of a stone she wore in a girdle. On this expedition of conquest, Empress Jingū's life was guarded by the *nigi-mi-tama* of Amaterasu while the *ara-mi-tama* of Amaterasu led her troops to victory.

---

* *Tama* also stands for a round ball or a jewel. Kato uses the phrase "jewel-breath."

Ikuta Jinja. Dedicated to Wakahirume-no-mikoto by the Empress Jingū after her return from three Korean kingdoms. The picture shows the sacred dance performed at the annual festival. (Kinki region.)

Nankō-sai. On May 25, a procession of about 1,000 of the parishoners of Minatogawa Jinja winds through the city of Kōbe. (Kinki region.)

So far as the old historical records are concerned, there is no reference to this "quiet soul" of Amaterasu's being at Ise Shrine. At the detached shrines at both Inner and Outer Shrines at Ise, her "rough soul" is enshrined. But there is no shrine dedicated specifically to her "quiet soul." Usually it is thought that the main shrine has the "quiet soul" as Amaterasu herself.

In the mythology of Shinto, the term "rough soul" occurs much more than the term "quiet soul." However, there are cases of shrines dedicated to the "quiet souls" of certain *kami*. For example, in the case of the kami Ō-Kuninushi who is enshrined at Izumo Taisha, his "quiet soul" is enshrined a long distance away, at Ō-Miwa Shrine, not far from Nara City. According to one of the ancient ritual prayers, he attached this peaceful spirit to a mirror of large dimensions and had it dwell in the sacred grove of Ō-Miwa.

Various interpretations have been made of the functions of the *ara-mi-tama* and the *nigi-mi-tama*. A very common interpretation, drawing its inspiration from Chinese thought, is that the *true nature* of the kami is *nigi-mi-tama*. When the *kami* starts to work outwardly, it is called *ara-mi-tama*. From the end of the Heian period this way of thinking became quite prominent, and it lasted up to the time of Motoori. According to this philosophy, the true nature or "quiet soul" stands for reality, substance. The *ara-mi-tama*, which is the working or action, is process or phenomena only. This interpretation is quite applicable to the case of Amaterasu at Ise, as the *nigi-mi-tama* is thought of as being Amaterasu herself. But it does not fit the case of Ō-Kuni-nushi, whose true nature is at Izumo while his *nigi-mi-tama* is at Ō-Miwa Shrine.

SACRIFICE IN SHINTO

It is significant that in the Shinto myth, no *kami* ever makes demands for sacrifices, whether animal or human. Most religious traditions reflect the feeling that only through the shedding of blood or the giving of a burnt sacrifice can man achieve his true good or goal. But Shinto *kami* do not demand offerings, the first-born of sons or of animals, even in the earliest traditions. Izanagi made no offerings when he cleansed himself after contacting pollution in Hades. He simply discarded his clothing and from them new creative forces sprang into existence, that is, more *kami*. There is no thought that pollution must be punished. It must simply be purified, washed away. The purification is what restores one to his essentially "right" nature. In very early times, the person who had contacted pollution probably brought what-ever things were regarded as polluted, and offered them so they could be thrown away in water. At least some of the rituals sur-viving into modern times lend themselves to this interpretation. Out of this practice may have developed the idea of demanding some kind of token payment as a penalty.[11]

By the seventh century or after, animal sacrifices either of horse or of cattle became a part of some rituals at certain places. These were probably the result of Chinese influence, and it never became a general practice. In the reign of Emperor Shōmu (701–756 A.D.), for seven years in a row a rich man sacrificed an ox to appease a wrathful Chinese deity. There are also cases of human sacrifice, to appease *kami* thought to be angry.[12] In the case cited in the *Nihonshoki,* one of the men "called the bluff" of the angry *kami* and the river was successfully dammed without his having to sacrifice himself.

Votive offerings of different kinds of weapons began in the reign of Emperor Suinin, according to the *Nihonshoki.* Today, the offering of votive tablets at shrines is quite common, made in connection with some specific petition to the *kami* such as the de-sire for a safe childbirth.

FOOD SYMBOLS AND LIFE SYMBOLS

Every religious tradition makes use of food symbols and symbols of life. The desire for "divine food" and "divine life"

Kasama Inari Jinja. The representative shrine in the Kantō region where the *kami* Inari is enshrined. Shrines to Inari are very popular among the people.

Ancient folk dance of the Suki region, at Munakata Jinja. (Kyushū region.)

have been expressed in myth, ritual, dogma, and architecture. The satisfaction of the hunger for daily bread and, later, the "food of immortality" lies near the center of every historical religion. The Great Mother, or the Mother Goddess as the divine breast, preceded the emergence of male symbols in the religions of mankind. An Indian Upanishad of over 2,500 years ago says, "From food all creatures are produced. . . . Food is the chief among beings. . . . Verily he obtains all food who worships Brahma as food. . . ."[13] The central rite of Christianity underscores the same emphasis. Mother Church provides the wine and the wafer which are the blood and the body of the god. Directed by the god himself, the believer takes and "eats."

In Shinto the protection of the food supply has always been an important aspect of the religious rituals. There are many *kami* associated with food. Inari, in popular stories associated with the fox, his messenger, is protector of the cultivation of rice and of other grains. Prayers and thanksgivings connected with agriculture are often offered to him. Rituals of imperial household Shinto, to be discussed in a later chapter, are also concerned with the food supply.

Not a part of Shrine Shinto but still present in many places in Folk Shinto are evidences of phallic worship. After 1868 many of the evidences of phallic worship in Folk Shinto were eliminated from public view, largely because the Meiji government was sensitive to the criticism of foreigners, nurtured in a religious tradition that regarded sexual symbols of the obvious sort as "improper." Cultures which have not associated aggravated guilt feelings with sexual symbols regard such symbols as natural and proper expressions of the fertility principle in life. The Shinto tradition does not downgrade sexuality nor is the sexual appetite regarded as wicked or sinful. In cultures shaped primarily by religions at the matriarchal level, it is the womb and the breast that are prominent, as in India where the lotus as the symbol of the womb is the source of all life. The ascetic sitting on the lotus throne also becomes the symbol of salvation or awakening. The patriarchal side of a religion expresses itself through the pillar or upright post, the male phallus. Such posts or upright stones used to be fairly common in rural Japan, an expression of Folk Shinto.

Only to a very minor extent do the Shinto myths themselves provide any basis for such phallic practices. In the account of Izanagi's flight from the underworld pursued by the female furies, at one point he flings down his staff saying, "The Thunders may not come beyond this." According to the *Nihonshoki* the staff was named "Pass-Not-Place-Kami" (Funado-no-kami).[14] The name is variously written in the Japanese. In one form, according to Holtom, the entire name stands for an obstruction of some sort, set against the ingress of evil. In another form it means "Crossroads Kami." In some places this *kami* was a very popular phallic *kami*.[15]

At the present time most of the festivals in Folk Shinto with an explicit phallic significance come in the spring of the year and are related to the desire for a good crop. At one place a large wooden male phallus is carried in a procession from the male shrine to the female shrine and then back again, with great rejoicing. At another rural shrine, much smaller, there is a marriage of two large ropes, one male and one female. At still another place in the Nara area, two men go through the motions of sexual intercourse on the shrine floor, one of the participants being dressed like a woman. This type of festival, however, is peripheral to Shrine Shinto.

One other type of guardian *kami* should be mentioned before we conclude our discussion of some of the types of *kami* in Shinto. These are the two Chimata-no-kami, or "Road Fork Kami," worshipped long ago in a festival called *Michi-ae-no-matsuri*, Festival of the Road Kami.[16] These two, who were occasionally thought of as husband and wife but ordinarily thought of as just male, would presumably keep back demons, evil spirits, or ghosts which haunted mountains, waters, and rocks. The festival dedicated to their worship was carried out at the four corners of the capital. A modern student of the prayer, or *norito*, central to this ancient festival, cannot help but feel there was a deeper psychological significance in the ritual than that of merely protecting the capital. This *norito* is preserved in the *Engishiki*, a writing of the tenth century during the Heian period.

> I humbly speak before the Sovereign Kami
> > Who dwell massively imbedded like sacred massed rocks
> > In the myriad great thoroughfares,
> > Whose praises are fulfilled by command of the
> > > Sovereign Grandchild:
>
> I humbly speak your names:
> > Ya-chimata-hiko,
> > Ya-chimata-hime,
> > Kunado,
> And fulfill your praises
>
> With the prayer that you will not be bewitched and will not
> > speak consent
> > To the unfriendly and unruly spirits
> > Who come from the land of Hades, the underworld;
> If they go below, you will guard below,
> > If they go above, you will guard above,
> > And will guard in the guarding by night and the guarding by
> > day,
> > And will bless.[17]

This seems to reflect an effort on the part of the worshippers to protect themselves from an uprush of mysterious forces coming from below the level of consciousness, lest they not be able to handle them. Hence the function of these *kami* should not be interpreted as having been exclusively magical, or as reflecting solely a desire to ward off demonic powers thought of as coming from mountains and caves. They also had a function in providing psychological controls over the forces of the instinctive life.

SOME GENERAL COMMENTS

The above summary should give some idea of the diversity in Shinto embraced by the term *kami*. *Kami* range all the way from spirits that can "possess" people, causing them to prophesy, to abstract *kami* who never appear in history except as names of founders of ancient houses. If a Westerner asks for the "systematic theology" of Shinto, he will probably be quite disappointed. Most of that theology is yet to be written. In the past, the need for it has been felt only occasionally and then only by some of the priestly schools and scholars. However, if Shinto today is to compete with other religious ideas, it will be forced to become more articulate theologically and philosophically. But Shinto arose without a founder and it expressed unconsciously a way of relating oneself to all the forces of nature. Concepts or ideas were not needed. There was no teacher trying to indoctrinate followers, asking them to believe him or to accept a revelation thought of as coming from a transcendent deity.

Shinto arose out of the attitudes and way of living of a people who were very much at home with their environment, first as hunters and fishers and then as tillers of the soil. The influence of this agricultural background has always been primary in Shinto rituals. The early Japanese realized intuitively how intimate was the reliance of man on nature. He was aware of the relativity of his daily life. He had no yearning for the absolute. He had no quarrel with the flesh. He had no craving for monism, such as India at one stage of her history was to develop almost to the point of an obsession. Japanese man knew the vagaries of nature with its typhoons, earthquakes, and volcanoes, but he never came to regard nature as essentially hostile or unfriendly. He never felt the tyranny of a desert sun nor did he visualize the torments of a hell. Patiently he sought to improve his cultivation of rice, feeling himself at home in nature. Such factors as these must have played a part in the emergence of thoughts and feelings so different from some of the leading thoughts of the Semitic religious tradition. Where the Semite came to feel alienated from his God and from the world of nature in a marked degree, the Japanese felt at home and on friendly relations.

Conspicuously absent from Shinto ideas of *kami* are notions of transcendence as developed by schools of thought in Christianity and Islam. Also absent are ideas of creation, monotheism,

omnipotence, and omniscience. So far as the question of omniscience is concerned, the myth indicates that whenever the
heavenly *kami* were faced with problems, they convened a council with Thought-Producer-Kami playing a prominent part, or
they held a divination to discover what course of action to take.

Similarly there is no concept of omnipotence or predestina-
tion. Appeal to overwhelming power has never been characteristic of Shinto, either in the myth or in its history. Related to this
is the absence of any idea of an Absolute whether in the form
of an Oriental despot or in the form of a philosophical Absolute.
The few exceptions to this occurred under Chinese influence. For
example, at the Outer Shrine of Ise, in the eleventh century, a
form of Shinto was developed under the influence of Buddhism
and Confucianism. In this "Ise Shinto," *kami* tended to become
absolute. This current recurs at points in some of the later schools
of thought, but it never became prominent in Shinto life for it
is not indigenous to Shinto. Shirai Soin wrote in 1670, "The
Deity is the Absolute. It transcends human words, which are of
a relative nature. It is incomprehensible and yet it permeates all
things. It is everywhere. People as a rule, not knowing this truth,
visit a hundred shrines day by day to worship there, and make
valuable offerings month by month, and yet they are not sure
to obtain any reward, though they may perchance suffer misfortunes in the world."[18]

Neither has the concept of transcendence had a central place
in Shinto experience. Westerners, as a consequence, have been
inclined to describe Shinto as a pantheism. But this, too, is a mistake, for there is some feeling for transcendence in Shinto, especially with reference to the heavenly *kami*, Ame-no-minaka-
nushi-no-kami. The heavenly *kami* are never visible to mankind.
Amaterasu is the *kami* who performs the rituals for them. Thus
the Shinto believer does conceive of divine factors which are beyond the world that can be perceived. However, the *kami* that he
is ordinarily concerned with are the *kami* that have actual relationship to his daily life.

Shinto, like all the religious traditions of mankind, includes within itself elements of animatism, animism, and magical practices, along with what is usually called polytheism. However, it is a mistake to use any of these terms simply to classify Shinto and thus dismiss it. For example, the word "polytheism" is not a word the average Shinto scholar would quibble about, for he admits the plurality of *kami* in Shinto. But Shinto is the kind of polytheism where all the *kami* are thought of as working together harmoniously, so that in effect the universe is just as unified as in the religions claiming to be monotheistic. Actually, in Shinto there is less of the sense of the universe being divided against itself than in orthodox Christian monotheism.

Fundamental to Shinto experience is the conviction that there is a *way of nature*, a cosmic way, according to which men should walk. That way is called *kami-no michi*, the Way of the Kami. This *michi* or way is akin to the way of philosophical Taoism. In fact, the character is the same though pronounced differently. In the more abstract terms of the Greek mind, this is *logos*. However, the Japanese mind was not the kind of mind that sought an abstract conceptual unity. The Japanese mind *felt* the unity. Feeling the unity, the Japanese was under no psychological compulsion to compensate at the conceptual level for what was lacking at the level of experience. This is not to suggest that all abstract thinking is compensatory in the sense that it is a substitute for more basic experiences; but often it comes perilously close to that.

If the basic mood or feeling of Shinto is to be put into philosophical terms, there are certain words which come fairly close to expressing it. In addition to the term *way* (*michi*), one should list that which unites or links together (*musubi*), as well as the terms growth, development, creation, improvement (*seisei hatten sōzō shinka*). All of these words have a dynamic connotation. They stand in the tradition of *process* philosophy rather than *substance* philosophy. Man is a finite being but he is capable of growth, creativity, and development. The evolutionary process is a *creative* process. *Kami* transcends man but *kami* is also operating within man, especially in his mind and heart (*kokoro*).

When it comes to the basic principles or convictions by which a person is living his life—*if* these are put into words at all, they are put into words that can be neither proved nor disproved. If they are honest words, not said just for an effect on listeners, they usually shade over into poetry or myth. In conclusion let me quote two poems written by Shinto priests, both of them formerly associated with the Great Shrine of Izumo.

> Deem not that only in this earthly shrine
> The deity doth reign.
> The earth entire, and all the Heavens Divine,
> His presence do proclaim!
>
> > Shima Shigeoyu

> No spot on earth but is a shrine—
> > Be it the vast expanse of ocean waste
> > Or highest mountain's summit, sun-caressed—
> In all resides the power divine.
>
> > Senge Takazumi[19]

CHAPTER FOUR

The Festivals of Shinto

It was a very cold night to be standing in a Shinto shrine. The temperature was only slightly above the freezing mark. Fortunately there was little wind. It was past midnight. A procession of white-robed Shinto priests filed silently from the shrine office. Two attendants were carrying a large wooden box with handles extending from each end. They proceeded to the purification area not far from the shrine path. The most solemn of all Shinto festivals upon which an outsider can gaze had begun. A Shinto scholar and I were the only persons present aside from the priests, who went about the purification rituals silently. A solitary night watchman stood nearby holding a paper lantern to provide a little light for the priestly activities.

This was the ritual of the autumn festival of thanksgiving, known as Kan-name-sai, and celebrated at the shrines of Ise. On the preceding day the first-fruits of the autumn harvest of grain had been offered at the Grand Shrine dedicated to Amaterasu as well as at the shrine dedicated to the food *kami* at the Outer Shrine of Ise. Now they were being offered at this shrine dedicated to the Moon Kami, Tsuki-yomi-no-kami.

Some of the rice fields around Ise still had rice plants standing in them, uncut. But most of the rice in the area had been harvested and the rice plants, with heavy ears of grain, were strung up on wooden bars at the edges of the rice paddies. Around the time of Kan-name-sai the wind smells like fall during the daytime, but at night it smells and feels like winter. It is the time of the changing of the seasons.

We watched the priests as they took their positions around the covered wooden box filled with the food offerings. A stick with white papers attached was waved over the box to purify it preparatory to the offering of the food. Then the priests resumed their procession across the cobblestones toward the inner shrine. The two attendants carried the box as before. A straw mat was placed on the stones not far from the steps that led to the door of the inner shrine. On this mat the head priest knelt. The other priests knelt at one side in a row at right angles to the head priest and the shrine. One torch was lit to provide light for the ceremony. The large food box was set down not far from the door of the shrine and was uncovered. The shrine door was slowly opened in preparation for the ritual of offering the food.

Step by ritual the ritual proceeded in total silence, broken only by the sound of the wooden shoes of the priests as they walked across the stones. First they carried small tables of food offerings to each of the four corners of the shrine building. Then they carried them to the head priest who placed them on the low tables at the top of the steep flight of steps just inside the opened door of the inner shrine. When the head priest read silently the ritual prayer from a scroll held in his hands, one attendant stood close by with the torch to enable him to see the ancient words which had been read in just this fashion for many centuries. This ceremony goes back at least two thousand years, probably more.

Standing in front of this shrine, built as a faithful copy of the many shrine buildings that had preceded it through the centuries, one was lifted out of the twentieth century into a timeless realm where one could sense the mystic potency which early agricultural man felt in the forces of nature. The offering of the food in this dignified fashion to the *kami* was a reminder of earlier people's constant remembrance that from nature, or the spirits in nature, comes all sustenance for which man should give thanks. Prior to the eighth century, the food thus offered to the *kami*, after being removed in the same slow, stately ritual, was served to all the participants in a common meal. This was a kind of physical communion with *kami* just as it also served as the bridge back from the solemn, sacred moments to the life of the ordinary world again. Nowadays, before they leave the shrine grounds worshippers often are given a drink of the rice wine or

Kan-name-sai. A festival of thanksgiving for the harvest celebrated on October 15-17 at the shrines of Ise. (Kinki region.)

Kan-name-sai. The picture shows the celebrants advancing.

sake which has been offered to the *kami*, a simplified version of the communion meal.

After the food had been offered to the *kami*, the trays of food were then returned to the large wooden box, one by one. When the ritual was completed, the box was carried from the Tsuki-yomi Shrine back to the nearby Outer Shrine of Ise, dedicated to the food *kami*. It was at the Outer Shrine that all of these food offerings had been prepared. The two attendants wearing ancient-style servant's clothing of white, followed by the attendant with the paper lantern, walked off with the large box through the dim shadows of the pine trees. Wrapping our own coats more tightly about us, we returned to the Japanese inn for a few hours of rest before a similar ritual would be repeated shortly after sunrise.

Many of the Shinto festivals have to do with the food supply. According to the *Records of Engi*, the annual Shinto rituals were classified under the headings Greater Festivals, Middle Festivals, and Lesser Festivals.[1] The Great Harvest Festival (Dai-jō-sai) stands alone in the first category. That is the occasion which comes only once in the reign of an emperor, when the emperor offers the new food at the time of his enthronement ceremony. The Middle Festivals include the festival of praying for a good harvest early in February, the monthly festivals, and the festival of the new rice crop. The Lesser Festivals include the festival of praying for abundant rice crops at the Hirose shrine, a festival for propitiating the wind *kami* in order to favor a rich harvest, a festival to appease the *kami* of epidemic diseases, a festival when the *sake* casks sacred to the *kami* are decorated with wild lily flowers, and the feast of the new rice crop preceding the one listed as a Middle Festival. The Lesser Festivals also include a soul-quieting ceremony, a festival for appeasing the Fire Kami, a festival of the road *kami*, and festivals associated with particular shrines.[2]

From time to time there have been Shinto priests or scholars who have tried to develop a Shinto theology. But on the whole Shinto has not endured through interpretations made by priests

Fire festival. The Fire Dance, performed to pray for protection from fire. Celebrated on December 16 at Akiba-San Hongū Akiba Jinja. (Chūbu region.)

Dragon dance. Performed in front of the portable shrine at the annual festival on May 5 at Nangū Jinja. (Chūbu region.)

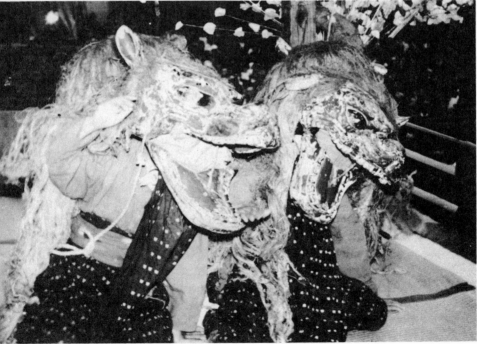

or priestly politicians, but through the traditional rituals and the feelings which they express and evoke. The festivals have been the main support of the life of Shinto and the priests have tried to keep the rituals as faithfully as possible. This is especially true of ancient shrines such as those at Izumo and Ise, but it also holds true at many other places. (Long before Ise was made sacred to Amaterasu, there was a shrine there at which traditional rituals were performed.)

Japanese scholars have attempted to discover what the word *matsuri* really means. In English it is usually rendered as "festival" or "ritual." According to one theory the word meant originally the act of a person in a lower position waiting upon a person in a higher position, or the younger serving the elder. Another interpretation finds the origin of the word in the term *matsu*, to wait. One awaits the *kami's* coming with food which will be offered to the *kami*. However, this explanation would not include the rituals of purification (*harae* and *misogi*). In purification, one is not inviting the *kami* or waiting with food. One is simply getting prepared for meeting the *kami*.

Another interpretation which has some plausibility traces the word *matsuri* to the word meaning to join, to be united or blended with (*mazaru-majiru*). What the ritual seeks to establish is a relationship between the human and the more-than-human. Man, related by birth to *kami*, seeks to go back to the state of *kami*, that is, to the *kami*-mind (*kami-no-kokoro*). *Kami* and the human being come to a more than usual intimacy, at least for the space of the festival. After the ritual is over, it is expected that one carries back with him into ordinary life the mind of the *kami*.

The Chinese characters for *matsuri* can also be pronounced *saishi*. The Chinese characters reveal more about the Chinese attitude toward deity than they do about the Shinto attitude toward the *kami*. The characters represent the offering of food, by one's hands, to deity on an altar. The food apparently was cooked pork, a favorite of the Chinese. In the case of Chinese deities, these food offerings were made to an angry deity of whom the worshippers were afraid. There is no such practice in traditional

Gion-matsuri of Hachiman Jinja. Pictured here is a procession through the city of Tobata with *yamagasa*. (Kyūshū region.)

Gion-matsuri. A celebration of Yasaka Jinja performed to pray for the dispelling of pestilence. Performed for twenty-eight days in July. The picture shows the procession of floats on July 17 in Kyoto. (Kinki region.)

Shinto rituals. There is a Shinto ritual called Hanashizume-no-matsuri, performed at Ō-Miwa and Sai Shrines, to the *kami* who protect people from diseases. And there is a festival directed to the *kami* of water whose purpose is to keep the *kami* of fire under control.³ Shinto *kami* are not wrathful as a rule. They are thought of more as parents. There is a folk story to the effect that in a certain village, the people believed that they had to offer a daughter each autumn to some *kami*. A brave man, dressed up like a woman, waited in the shrine, convinced that no *kami* would make such a demand. Apparently his experiment was quite successful and convincing. The feelings underlying the basic Shinto festivals are friendly feelings, not a mood of fear.

In very ancient times Shinto rituals were probably strongly influenced by the practices of shamanism when a man or a woman (and in Japan, it was more often a woman) became "*kami*-possessed." While in that state of possession, oracles or revelations were propounded by the shaman or medium concerning the weather, prospects for the crops, or courses of action which the villagers should take. In such cases a specific type of response was expected from the *kami*. In later periods, it was the mind of *kami* which the worshipper expected to receive. There was a two-way communication of a sort, with the priest sometimes centrally involved. Very little is known about the details of the ancient rituals. After the influx of Chinese influence many Shinto ceremonies were modified, especially by some of the practices of Taoism at its popular or folk level. (The Great Food Festival, Dai-jō-sai, which will be discussed in a later chapter, seems to have been the only ritual influenced very little by China.)

Broadly speaking, there are five purposes expressed in the various types of rituals. The type most frequent among the common people is the ritual pertaining to requests made to the *kami* by people wanting such things as sons or a good rice crop or good health. The second type of festival is an expression of thanks to *kami* for benefits or graces already bestowed. A third purpose of rituals is to pacify or soothe *kami* who might otherwise be violent or destructive. Tradition provided rituals also for pacifying souls which might place a curse on living persons. These types of rituals

Chōna-Hajime-sai. On January 11, carpenters assemble at Oguni Jinja and perform a ceremony of the first use of the adze (*chōna*) of the New Year. (Chūbu region.)

Procession honoring the tutelary *kami* of Sasebo City. Winds through the city on three days from November 1-3. (Kyūshū region.)

occur every day in Japan. Two other types of festivals which oc-
cupy an important place in Folk Shinto are magical rituals and
festivals of divination. These have always played an important
part in the life of the peasants. They occur very rarely in Shrine
Shinto but are still prevalent in Folk Shinto.

There are also rituals of the imperial household which belong to the first three types mentioned above. We shall discuss
some of them separately later. These rituals have been guided
since early times by rules.[4] For the special rituals of individual
shrines and for the magical rituals, there are no rules.

PREPARATIONS FOR THE RITUALS

For the usual festival there are three stages—the preparation, the *matsuri* proper, and the return to everyday life. The
head priest who will officiate at the ritual prepares himself by a
form of abstinence or avoidance (*kessai*). To be sure of having
a clean body before worshipping the *kami*, the priest must avoid
touching polluted objects or persons. To make this possible, he
has to abstain from many kinds of activities and from certain
kinds of food which are too spicy. Also, for a period immediately
preceding the main ceremony he shuts himself up alone in a special room of the shrine. For a big festival in earlier periods, the
number of days of avoidance was quite long; for a smaller festival,
the period was just a few days.

There are two kinds of avoidance. The one called "rough
avoidance" is of a more general nature. In ancient times, in preparation for the Great Food Festival, it lasted three months. Later
it was reduced to one month. The other type of avoidance is called
"strict avoidance" and used to last for three days. During the
"rough avoidance" the priest could attend to regular shrine business, including participating in the ceremonial music and dancing, *bugaku*, which is a part of the worship at many of the larger
shrines which can afford it. However, during the "strict avoidance" the priest could take no part in shrine affairs nor could he

drink *sake,* the rice wine. For three days he remained in his room taking frequent baths. The other priests at the shrine had to take care of the usual shrine business of getting ready for the crowds at the festival.

Among the various preparations in which the assistant priests are engaged is the arranging of the meal which will be served to the *kami.* Elaborate care is taken that no pollution touch the food. At one of the ancient shrines we were allowed to enter the special room where the food was being prepared. The fire for the cooking was started in the ancient fashion by one of the priests striking a piece of metal against stone. The tiny sparks were allowed to fall upon thin wood shavings in a special box. When these ignited, they were carefully transferred to the fire-box beneath the rice container. Other foods, both cooked and un-cooked, were carefully arranged on the small table-trays. The priest wore a mask over his mouth and nose in this particular shrine so that he would not breathe directly onto the food he was arranging.

This food for *kami* (known as *shin-sen*) can be of two kinds, raw and cooked. But it is of first importance that no blood show on any of the uncooked food, whether chicken, fish, or deer meat. In China, when sacrifices were made to the gods, it was quite ac-ceptable for blood to show. But in Shinto, blood is pollution, so when meat is used, it is very carefully prepared. *Sake* is also part of the meal served to *kami.* The ancient *sake* was not clear like today's *sake.* Often it was allowed to ferment only one or two nights before being offered to *kami.* Even though sour the *sake* was enjoyed by the *kami* as well as by the worshippers.

The people who come to participate in the festival also un-dergo some form of purification. This is to get rid of any pollu-tions that one may have contacted consciously or unconsciously. In earlier centuries the purification was literally a more thorough physical cleansing than it is today; it involved the use of water (*misogi.*) One went to a place where a river emptied into the sea and there washed his entire body. The traditional basis for this is the story in the myth of Izanagi's purification after his return from the underworld. After Kyoto was made the capital, a practical problem presented itself since Kyoto was quite far from the sea. Instead, the Kamo River which flows through present-day Kyoto but which used to be to the east of it, was used. In early times, even the emperor went to the river for part of his purification before participating in the Great Food Festival.

Today at almost any Shinto shrine one finds facilities for the *te-mizu* ceremony when one pours water over his hands and rinses out his mouth. Near the entrance to the shrine is a spot, usually roofed over, where there is running water where one can perform this ablution. At some ceremonies today salt water is sprinkled over the participants. Also people who have been to a funeral sprinkle salt on themselves before re-entering their homes, if they follow the traditions. The little piles of salt that one may see at the entrance to some restaurants are the result of Shinto influence, a modern reminder of the part that the sea and its water once played in the purification rites.

There is another form of purification, done without water, called *harai* (or *harae*, the older term). This is done by the waving of a stick to which have been attached pieces of linen cloth or irregularly cut pieces of white paper. A branch of the sakaki tree, an evergreen tree sacred to Shinto, may be used in the same way. The priest waves the implement to the left, to the right, and then back again to the left. This accomplishes the same result as purification by water. The abstinence on the part of the head priest, the purification by water or by the waving of the wand, are all a part of the preparation for approaching *kami*. They are not the goal of the ceremony. (In a later chapter we shall see how purification became an end in itself for some groups, leading even to the practice of self-mummification.)

THE CENTER OF THE FESTIVAL

In ancient times the festivals occurred at night. They began in the evening and ended about dawn. In the Heian period this was still the rule, but in the Kamakura period the custom changed.

Fire kindling. In order to obtain a pure fire, fire is kindled by standing a stick of *sakaki* wood upon a board of *hinoki* wood and rubbing them together. (Kinki region.)

Futami Okitama Jinja. Located on the Futami-ga-ura coast of Ise. Most people who worship at Ise Jingu also worship here. There is a custom of worshipping the rising sun through the *shimenawa* rope which is strung between two rocks. (Kinki region.)

With the ascendancy of the warrior class, the festivals began to occur more frequently in the daytime. Various theories are offered as to the reason for the change of time. One theory is that originally there were no people who went to a festival to watch it. They went as participants. But once people began to go to festivals more to watch or enjoy them, the time of the festival shifted to the day. There may have been other reasons also. So far as the feast after the festival was concerned, in the eighth century the government issued orders forbidding it at night on the grounds that along with the joyous drinking went too much immorality. This could have been a factor in forcing the change of time for the entire festival.[5]

The center of the festival in ancient times was the inviting of the *kami* to come down and take up its residence temporarily in the sacred place. In very early times there were no shrine buildings. The *kami* came down to a purified place marked off by sacred straw-rope and evergreens. The tree which stood in the middle of this was called *himorogi*, a tree from which the leaves did not fall.[6] Around the sacred spot were placed stones. Today in Japan there are only a few places left where this type of worship outside the shrine is still celebrated. On the island of Kyushu at Munakata Shrine, we climbed the hill back of the shrine buildings to the spot where for many centuries past, the *kami* has been worshipped outdoors. The simplicity of the sacred spot and the quietness of the natural surroundings made us realize how buildings dedicated to religious purposes tend to cut one off from the human attachment to the natural environment. The beauty of a Gothic cathedral has one message about how man conceives his relationship to the invisible realities; the ornateness of a Buddhist temple has another message. But the simplicity and directness of a Shinto shrine open to the skies, the trees, and the weather has a message of a different sort which city dwellers find hard to understand.

In the *Nihonshoki* the origin of the *himorogi*, or sacred outdoor shrine, is traced back to the divine ages, to the time when the heavenly grandson, Ninigi-no-mikoto, descended to earth. Taka-mi-musubi-no-kami says there: "I will set up the heavenly *himorogi* and the heavenly *iwasaka* (rock boundary) wherein to practice religious abstinence on behalf of my descendants." To two of the other *kami* he says: "Take with you the heavenly *himorogi*, and go down to the Central Land of Reed-Plains . . . and you will there do religious rituals on behalf of my descendants."[7]

Thus the earliest place for Shinto worship of the *kami* seems to have been an enclosed area purified and marked off with stones, with a sakaki tree in the center onto which the *kami* was invited to descend for the festival. Standing at one of these spots which has been protected against the encroachments of commercialism, one begins to understand what the twelfth century poet felt when he wrote:

> What is enshrined I do not know
> But the awe of a sense of gratitude
> Brings tears to my eyes.[8]

When shrine buildings became the custom, the *kami* was thought of as residing within the inner shrine. This inner sanctuary (called *honden*) is the holy of holies where only priests may enter. In this sanctuary is the *go-shintai*, the object of worship in which the spirit of the *kami* is believed to reside. This may be a mirror kept covered, a stone, a sword, a sacred text, a spearhead, or some other object. The ordinary person is not allowed to touch or look at this holy object. (In those few cases where the sacred object is a statute of the Buddha, it is open to view.)

The ritual of opening the door of the inner shrine reflects the ancient practice of inviting the *kami* to come down to the sacred place outdoors. The head priest utters a long, deep "oh . . ." sound. The priest then bows at the foot of the steps leading up to the shrine and the ceremonial offering of the meal begins. The food is presented on small, unpainted table-stands which are carried at eye-level by the priests, being passed slowly from one priest to the next and at the end of the line being handed to the head priest, who ascends the steps to the sanctuary. He places the small stands on low tables in front of the object which symbolizes the presence of the *kami*. The vegetables, fish, rice, and *sake* are all prepared in beautiful arrangements.

Kagura. A Kagura performance called Miko-mai (dance of the priestesses). Kagura dances are still performed frequently at the shrines which can afford them. (Chūbu region.)

Tōkei-gaku and *Jindai-odori.* An ancient Kagura dance performed by the *uji-ko* at the annual festival of Minashi Jinja in September. (Chūbu region.)

After all the food has been placed on the tables in front of the *kami*, the head priest kneels at the foot of the steps and intones an ancient prayer (called *norito*). These ritual prayers recited by the priest are in archaic style and form a part of Japan's most ancient literature.[9] The prayers have to do with hopes for an abundant crop, protection from damage caused by wind and water, petition for the removal of sins or pollution, protection for the imperial household, thanksgiving, and so on. The type of *norito* read is determined by the type of ceremony itself. The chanting of the prayer is the central item in the festival. (In ancient times at a divination ritual, a reply was expected directly from the *kami*, through the priest or shaman.)

When the prayer has been chanted to its end, the *kami* is again worshipped, all the priests bowing down to the floor. Then music and dance, known as *kagura*, follow. There are two types of dance. One is classical in form and is expressed most fully in the music and dancing handed down in the imperial court. The other is "village *kagura*," handed down among the people. The music and dance are to give pleasure to the *kami* but undoubtedly the worshippers enjoy it also. The mythical origin of this dancing goes back to the occasion in heaven when Amaterasu withdrew into a cave because of the outrages committed by her violent brother, Susanoo. The other *kami* put on a music and dance performance in order to entice her back into the outer world. The original heavenly dance included some striptease, but that is not reflected in the classical *kagura* nor in the village dances. Since *kagura* is rather expensive to put on, the smaller shrines cannot afford it. The larger shrines have a separate building near the main shrine where the young girls, called *miko*, dance in stately style, wearing attractive garments of white and red. The dance building is open on two or three sides so all may enjoy the dancing.

After the music and dancing, the food is removed in the same manner as it was brought in, beginning this time with the head priest removing each table-stand individually from the low tables in front of the sacred object. When all the food has been removed, the head priest repeats the long-drawn-out "oh . . ." sound. The door to the inner shrine is shut. The main part of the ritual is over.

Sword dance. A heroic dance performed at the Kagura-sai festival in the spring at Ōasahiko Jinja. (Shikoku region.)

Procession festival held on October 15 (old calendar) at Bōtu Temmangū. On this day thousands of believers join the procession clad in white costumes. (Chūgoku region.)

TRANSITION TO ORDINARY LIFE

The third stage of the festival is to return the participants to the normal conditions prevailing before the festival began. The tension engendered by the contact with *kami* must be released. This takes place at an after-feast called *naorai*. The food and drink which have been offered to the *kami* are now consumed by the believers. This is a communion meal between *kami* and people. In ancient Japan, to eat together by dipping into the common pot or kettle meant that one belonged to the same clan or family. That is, it meant acceptance. This after-feast is also in the nature of a party, an occasion of gaiety through which one returns to ordinary everyday life. The after-feast is not common now though at certain festivals at many shrines, one drinks the *sake* which has been offered to the *kami*. The assistant priests offer each person a shallow cup into which the cold *sake* is poured, and it is drunk by the participant immediately. At some special festivals the shrine also provides a box lunch for the participants, but these lunches are usually taken away from the shrine to be eaten.

When individuals go to a shrine to worship, they may offer to the *kami* a small branch of the evergreen sakaki to which strips of white paper have been attached. This is called *tamagushi*. Two interpretations of what this means should be mentioned. One which is common among those who follow the Shinto scholar Motoori Norinaga, is that *tama* means jewel and *kushi* (*gushi*) means stick. Motoori claimed that this was something given to the *kami* as a present. The other school of thought claims that Motoori simply reveals here how little he knew about actual shrine teachings. At Izumo, for example, the *tamagushi* is not a present but a form of worshipping through which the worshipper seeks to be united with the *kami*. *Tama* stands for soul (*tamashii*) and *kushi* stands for that which links together. When one offers the sakaki branch to the *kami*, the stem is made to point toward the *kami* in the shrine. This indicates the worshipper's desire to return to the *kami* mind. Before offering it, one bows twice with the hope of receiving the *kami* mind. In effect, one places his own

Heian Jingū. Enshrines the first Emperor to reign in Kyoto, Emperor Kammu, as well as the last, Emperor Kōmei. The shrine building is built as a replica of the Daigokuden, one of the buildings in the ancient Heian Capital.

Ceremonial cooking. Fish is prepared according to ancient prescriptions to present to the *kami* at Hōkoku Jinja. (Kinki region.)

soul on the sakaki branch and offers it to *kami*. Clapping the hands after the presentation is to show spiritual agreement or understanding. This is the interpretation of the actions which the priests at Izumo Shrine have been following through the centuries.* At all shrines the procedures are as just given, but interpretations vary.

THE EMPEROR AND RITUALS

In ancient times the connection between Shinto and the imperial court was very intimate. One word stood both for rituals and for government, *matsuri-goto*, "ritual affairs."· The term *miya* stood for shrine and for the imperial court also. The word for imperial palace, *kyūjō*, is composed of two Chinese characters, the first meaning shrine and the second meaning castle.** Until the tenth emperor, Sujin (97-30 B.C.), the residence of the emperor was also the shrine of his divine ancestors. From the time of the emperor Jimmu, whose legendary date of 660 B.C. is probably at least six centuries too early, to the present emperor, one of the main responsibilities of the imperial house has been its part in Shinto rites and ceremonies. "National Shinto," the artificial promotion of the Meiji government, built upon this ancient custom when it indoctrinated the people in the last quarter of the nineteenth century with the doctrine of the "unity of religious rites and politics" (*saisei itchi*), with the emperor as divine. Let us look at some of the rituals of the imperial household.

These rituals, fundamental ones in Shinto, are performed among all the *kami* and the emperor has the highest position by the emperor himself. Amaterasu has the highest position

---

* The clapping of hands to show spiritual understanding was later adapted to daily life. When an agreement was concluded, the agreeing parties clapped their hands. At one of the Shinto festivals which a Japanese friend and I attended in Asakusa in Tokyo, whenever a shop sold a sacred memento to a buyer, all concerned would clap their hands in rhythm, showing agreement had been reached.

** The word *jinja* for shrine is the modern term. *Miya* or *o-miya* is the older term and the more popular term in common usage. The term *jinja* means *kami* dwelling place and *miya* means honorable house.

among the Japanese. Hence he must perform them or direct them. Modernization, Westernization and the Allied Occupation in the months following August, 1945, have not changed these patterns. Since 1945 the rituals of the imperial household have been called private affairs rather than affairs of state. This means that all of the expenses for them are taken out of the private means of the imperial household. But in no sense did the defeat or the Occupation or the new constitution sever the emperor's connection with Shinto. Legally speaking Shinto is now only the "private belief" of the imperial household; it is not an affair of government. Many of the younger generation in Japan today know little about Shinto and the place that Shinto rituals play in the life of the emperor. But as far as the older generation's feelings are concerned, especially those who live in the country and the villages, the postwar legal changes probably mean little.

Since the time of Emperor Meiji when the capital was removed from Kyoto to Tokyo, the place for performing most of the imperial household rituals is the *Sanden,* or Three Shrines, grouped together southwest from the emperor's residence in the direction of Ise where the Grand Shrine of Amaterasu is located. The middle of the Three Shrines is the *Kashikodokoro.* In it is kept a mirror just like the one at Ise Shrine. According to myth and tradition, when Ninigi came down to earth, he was given Three Sacred Treasures—a mirror, a sword, and some jewels. Ninigi was told to regard the mirror as though it were Amaterasu herself. The *Kojiki* states that this mirror was the one used to lure Amaterasu out of her rock cave after she had hidden herself. The sword was the one obtained by Susanoo, Amaterasu's unruly brother, when he killed the eight-headed serpent at the headwaters of a river in Izumo. The jewels are described as being of the length of eight hands, five hundred in all. These Three Sacred Treasures are the symbols of imperial authority. According to the Imperial Household Law which has operated for many centuries, no emperor is truly emperor unless he possesses these emblems.[10]

The first human emperor, Jimmu, kept the mirror in his own residence. Until the time of the tenth emperor this remained the case. However, Sujin saw the country undergo a great pestilence

Udo Jingū. Enshrines the father of the first Emperor, Jimmu. Located in the cave where legend says that the *kami* was born. (Kyūshū region.)

Udo Jingū. The Main Shrine (Honden) located inside the cave. (Kyūshū region.)

shortly after the beginning of his reign. Fearing the possible pollution of the sacred emblems and wanting to show full respect
to Amaterasu, he had copies made of the mirror and the sword.
Thereafter, he kept only these replicas in the palace, along with
the original jewels. The sword and mirror were removed to Ka-
sanui in Yamato, where a shrine was built for them. He sent his
own daughter, Princess Toyosuki Iri-hime, to be in charge of the
worship of the shrine, with the command that she was to guard
the treasures with her life. During the reign of the next emperor,
Suinin (29 B.C. to 70 A.D.), the treasures were moved again,
coming to rest at Ise at the present Inner Shrine. One of the emperor's daughters was appointed priestess charged with their
worship, and this became customary.[11]

The sword was used extensively by the twelfth emperor's
son when he was fighting the eastern provinces which were in
revolt. He also took the sword with him on his fight in the area
of Kantō, the general region around present-day Tokyo. While
crossing the rough sea at the entrance to Tokyo Bay, a storm sud-
denly came up whereupon his wife jumped into the waves to calm
them. Later the prince was fighting serpents near Lake Biwa but
he had forgotten to take the sword along. Being badly wounded
he returned to a place called Atsuta and there he died. A shrine
was built for the sword there, and at this Atsuta Shrine the sword
is presently to be found.

Presumably the Three Sacred Treasures held today are the
same as those of ancient times. However, the replicas have had
some misfortunes befall them. The replica of the mirror has been
damaged by fire several times, in 960 in a palace fire and again
in 1005 when it was almost totally destroyed, only a small portion remaining. Another fire in 1040 damaged the fragment so
badly that it was reduced to very small fragments. It is these fragments that are kept in the *Kashikodokoro* of the imperial palace.
The original has stayed at Ise.[12]

While in early times their magical power was probably primary, many centuries ago they took on a symbolical significance
with ethical overtones. In the fourteenth century Kitabatake
Chikafusa (1293-1354) wrote in his history of Japan:

The Mirror reflects from its bright surface every object as it really is, irrespective of goodness or badness, beauty or the reverse. This is the very nature of the Mirror, which faithfully symbolizes truthfulness, one of the cardinal virtues. The Jewel signifies soft-heartedness and obedience, so that it becomes a symbol of benevolence. The sword represents the virtue of strong decision, i.e. wisdom. Without the combined strength of these three fundamental virtues, peace in the realm cannot be expected.[13]

The center building of the Three Shrines in the imperial palace grounds, the *Kashikodokoro*, is the place where the replica mirror is now kept. The building immediately to the left, called the *Kōreiden*, enshrines the souls of all the previous emperors as well as the souls of their consorts. The building to the right is called the *Shinden* and in it are enshrined all the *kami*. Prior to the time of Emperor Meiji, the counterpart of this building in the old capital of Kyoto was called *Hasshin-den* because eight *kami* (*has-shin*) were enshrined in it. Besides these three sanctuaries, there are some other buildings close by that play a part in the various rituals of the imperial household.

The number of regular imperial household rituals a year is sixty-four. Besides these, there are other special ones. According to the Imperial Household Law of Rituals which still operates (though unofficially) since the end of the war in 1945, there are thirteen major rituals which the emperor himself must perform. There are many others when the emperor is supposed to be present, and still others when he can send someone in his place. According to a former ritualist of the imperial palace, the emperor is performing rituals about one-sixth of the year.

The imperial household ritual of the opening of the new year is a good illustration. New Year's is a very important event in Japanese life. It involves cleaning the house thoroughly, preparing the food for the three-day holiday, paying back all old debts or obligations. On the second and third days it involves a great deal of visiting. It also touches some deeper dimensions in the Japanese which seem to be more or less religious in nature. At Meiji Shrine in Tokyo, well before midnight thousands of peo-

Kamo Wakeikazuchi Jinja. From antiquity the object of worship by the Imperial House. Tutelary *kami* of the Heian Capital, Kyoto. (Kinki region.)

Hirano Jinja. The tutelary *kami* of Kyoto City; was moved here in the year 794 from Nagaoka. (Kinki region.)

ple start walking into the shrine by way of the numerous path-
ways that thread their way through the surrounding parkland
or outer gardens. There is a constant stream of masses of people,
one-half of the crowd flowing in while the other half flows out.
Along the path on which we were moving around 2:00 a.m., there
were stationed many police to handle the crowds. Periodically
there were bonfires in the middle of the path, tended by Boy
Scouts. Moving along very slowly with the crowd, I wondered
how to assess its mood. What currents were moving below the
surface to bring a million and a quarter people to this one shrine
in three days, it was impossible to know. As the crowds at the
shrine building milled and shoved to get as close to the inner
sanctuary as the police line permitted, I found myself watching
the policemen who stood with arms linked together in front of
the area where the ten-yen pieces were being tossed by celebrants.
Most of them wore eye-protectors to protect their eyes from the
coins thrown not too accurately from some distance back in the
crowd. Were the other participants in a more religious mood than
I, I wondered?

While all this pushing, shoving, and throwing of coins was
going on, over in the imperial palace grounds preparations were
quietly going ahead for the private ritual of the emperor. These
preparations are carried out at the *Kashikodokoro*. At 5:10 a.m.
the emperor purifies himself carefully and changes into his special clothing for the rituals. Then he walks out into the garden
where a temporary structure has been erected, about twenty-four
feet square. He sits down on the matting and a screen is put
around him so no one can see the rituals. Then he begins the
worship of the *kami* in all directions, *Shi-Hō-Hai*, literally, "Four
Directions Worship." First he worships the Grand Shrine of Ise,
then various other shrines. This includes the mausoleum of Jimmu Tennō, first emperor, the Atsuta Shrine which has the divine
sword, and several shrines dedicated to the heavenly *kami*.

This worshipping in the four directions is probably the result of Chinese influence. In China when a new king took the
throne, he was expected to perform rituals to all the deities in the
world. It is quite probable that the original form of Japanese wor-

ship at the beginning of the year was simply the worshipping of the Kami of the Harvest, to insure a good harvest for the year.

The ritual of worshipping the *kami* in all directions takes about ten minutes. Then *Saitansai* begins. The emperor leaves the temporary structure and goes to the *Kashikodokoro* of the Three Shrines. Alone, he enters the inner room where Amaterasu is enshrined. No one can see what goes on in there. After offering to the *kami* the *go-hei*, the stick with paper or cloth attached, it is said that there is a bell-ringing ceremony. According to priests who have heard the bell, the sound is very clear and pleasing in tone. No explanation is given of this ceremony except that through it, the mind of the *kami* is known by the emperor. The emperor then goes to the two adjoining buildings and repeats the same ritual. This concludes the ritual of thinking about the beginning of the country and of worshipping the ancestors. A new year has been opened with the appropriate Shinto ceremonies in the imperial household.

CHAPTER FIVE

The Emperor and the Great Festival of New Food

Every year the Japanese people and their emperor celebrate a Festival of New Food, Nii-name-sai, when the first-fruits are offered as a thanksgiving for the harvest.[1] The emperor celebrates this festival on November 23 and 24, not only offering some of the year's first grain harvest but also partaking of it himself. This ritual is at least as old as the days when Japan moved out of a purely hunting and fishing culture into an agricultural culture, with rice and other grains becoming the main staple food. This festival of thanksgiving was an annual occasion when the first rice was offered to the *kami*. According to the Shinto myth, in the divine ages Amaterasu performed the festival in the Plain of High Heaven. Then when she sent her grandson down to rule the world, Ninigi's wife Adatsu-hime performed the same ritual. These legends from the distant past were tied in with the legends and myths of the Yamato ruling house as it extended its sway over the island. In any event, the common people as well as the emperor had, at a very early time, an annual harvest festival. In the case of the emperor, he himself served as the chief priest, just as his divine ancestress had served in that role in heaven. The *Manyōshū*, which comes from the Nara period, has poems which describe the New Food Festival of the common people.

Formerly this annual festival was called *Dai-jō-sai*, Great Food Festival, and when it was performed immediately after the accession of a new emperor, it was termed *Senso Dai-jō-sai*, Great Festival of New Food at the Accession. Now the term *Dai-jō-sai* is reserved exclusively for the occasion when a new emperor first offers the new food to Amaterasu and other *kami*. By performing this ritual, the emperor becomes emperor in fact as well as in name.[2] In ancient times the public accession to the throne also took place at this time. It seems that everybody participated in this event. The written records are unclear as to when the enthronement ceremony was separated from the Great Festival of New Food.[3]

There have been only a few occasions when this important Shinto ritual has not been performed by a new emperor. In the fifteenth century, society fell into great disorder. The military class became quite unruly and the income of the court nobles practically disappeared. For about one hundred years there was no Great Festival of New Food on the accession of new emperors because of the poverty of the court nobles and the emperor. When the Tokugawa family came to power and the power of the military government increased, the Tokugawas did what they could to restrict the power and influence of the emperors. Consequently they prohibited the performance of *Dai-jō-sai* for another one hundred years. However, people close to the emperor in Kyoto began to insist that Japan was the kind of country that, in its very nature, had to perform this ritual. The Tokugawa were forced to yield to this pressure, and with the emperor Higashiyama they permitted the Great Festival of New Food to be held, in 1687. Since money for it was still scarce, its scale was about half that of the ones in the early period. With the following emperor, the military government prohibited the Great Festival once more, but that was the last time they could prevent its being held. Since the time of Emperor Sakuramachi, the Great Festival has been held for each new emperor.

When direct imperial rule was restored with the accession of Emperor Meiji to the throne in 1868, the last Tokugawa military ruler having resigned, the capital was transferred from Kyoto to Tokyo and the Great Festival of New Food was performed in Tokyo for the first time, on December 28, 1871. According to the "Rules for Accession to the Throne," issued in 1909, just a few years before Emperor Meiji's death, the Great Festival must hereafter always be held in Kyoto. The emperor was aware of the distress of the people of Kyoto who had lost the emperor from their midst after centuries of history, and this was an attempt to maintain something of the ancient glory of Kyoto.

Another change resulting from the 1909 accession rules is that the enthronement ceremony and the Great Festival of New Food must be done in succession. Formerly, the enthronement ceremony could take place any time of the year. Now it must immediately precede the Great Festival which is a fixed autumn festival. For Emperor Taishō, who acceded to the throne in 1912, the rule of 1909 was followed. For Emperor Hirohito, the present emperor, who came to the throne in 1926, these rules plus some modifications made by the imperial household on December 30, 1927, were followed.

PRESENT-DAY *DAI-JŌ-SAI*

The present-day Great Festival of New Food includes not only the very ancient Shinto practices for guarding the food supply, but also the application of the most modern scientific knowledge regarding the cultivation of rice. Central to the ancient ritual itself is the mystery of the growth process, the importance of guarding the seed from year to year, and the communing with the invisible forces or *kami*. Yet the old and the new mingle in the rites without any sense of contradiction.

First is the matter of choosing the exact date for the festival. In the fall of the year preceding the year in which the Great Festival is to be held, a temporary office is established for all the officials who will be involved, and the date is determined by consultation. This date is then reported to the *kami* of the Three Shrines in the palace grounds. The same report is made at Ise Shrine, at the tomb of the first emperor, and at the tomb of the immediately preceding emperor. After this ceremony is completed, the districts in which the rice fields are to be chosen are decided by the ancient practice of divination.

O-taue-sai. Field-planting ceremony held June 10 every year at Kasama shrine. (Kantō region.) Inari shrines are closely associated with the production of food.

O-taue-sai. Rice-planting dance performed by maidens before the shrine on July 7 at Fuji-San Hongū Sengen Jinja. (Chūbu region.)

The method of divination in very early times was probably through the use of deer bones. Such practice is now rare, though at Nukisaki Shrine the shoulder bone of a deer is still used in divination. Divination by tortoise shell became the custom in the imperial house a long time ago, presumably when the Urabe family brought this Chinese method of divination to the court. The divination ceremony for determining the two districts in which the rice for the Great Festival should be grown, took place for the present emperor at the Imperial Palace on February 5, 1928. A temporary structure of thatch was constructed in front of the shrine to the right of the *Kashikodokoro*, that is, the *Shinden* or shrine dedicated to the *kami* of heaven and earth. Within this shelter, on a small wooden table, a *himorogi* was placed, that is, the sacred sakaki tree with streamers of hemp and paper attached to it. In front of the divination shelter, clean sand was spread. The actual divination took place here after the worship of the *kami* of heaven and earth had been completed.

At the divination ceremony, two *kami* of divination are invited to come down to the sacred tree. While soft music is played, a ritualist who has undergone extensive purification rites kindles a fire by rubbing together two pieces of wood. After the sparks have ignited the specially prepared wood, he holds a tortoise shell over the flames until it is cracked. Lines have already been drawn on the shell and several characters have been inscribed. From the reading of the cracks the ritualist discovers the will of the *kami* as to the two districts from which the specific rice fields will be chosen. He writes this down on a paper which is sealed and placed in a box before the sacred tree in the shelter. Following some more music, the *kami* are allowed to return to heaven and the box is handed over to the chairman of the Enthronement Commission. He reads the report and tells the results to the Prime Minister, who reports in turn to the emperor.

The manner of reading has been kept a secret within one family. When the ritualist who performed this divination ceremony for Emperor Hirohito was asked by a Japanese authority on Shinto how it was done, he replied that he could not reveal this to anyone outside the family authorized to do it. He can

Nukisaki Jinja. Enshrines the *kami* of the development of the land of Kōzuke. Divination through the use of a deer shoulder bone is still practised at this shrine. (Kantō region.)

Sticking paste to a pole. Rice paste is smeared on a pole about three yards high; according to how well it sticks, the state of the crops during the year is divined. (Tōhoku region.)

pass the secret on to only one person before he dies, to someone descended from the ancient Urabe family. Why this has to be kept a secret, known only within the Urabe family, is not indicated in any of the histories.

According to tradition, one of the districts chosen for the divine rice field is supposed to be east of Kyoto, and the other to the west of Kyoto. The district to the east is called Yuki-no-Kuni and the one to the west is called Suki-no-Kuni. Two fields are required because the central ceremonies of the Great Festival are carried out in identical buildings which reproduce the simple architecture of the dwellings of emperors in ancient Japan. One is called the Yuki Den and the other building is called the Suki Den.[4] The meaning of these two words is not clear, but it is possible that *yuki* originally meant "consecrated-purified" or "tabooed-purified." Whether *suki* should be interpreted as *tsugi*, "next," in modern Japanese, is more debatable.[5]

In modern times, after the will of *kami* has been determined by divination, the National Department of Agriculture and Forestry steps in with some wise precautions and regulations. The fields chosen in each district must belong to rural families who have adequate property and sound health. The land must be capable of being cultivated as one piece and be about one-fourth of an acre in size. It must be near a river so that the Shinto rituals of purification can be carried out easily. Drainage and irrigation must be good. It should be in an area protected as far as possible from the dangers of floods and storms. It must be in a district that is advanced in agricultural knowledge and techniques, as well as having a reputation for benevolence and good manners. Areas that have recently had epidemics must be avoided. No manure may be used as fertilizer. The men and women who are selected to cultivate the crops must wear unsoiled garments. The fields themselves are protected by the erection of bamboo mats on all sides and high fences of interwoven bamboo. Everything used in the cultivation of rice is purified by Shinto rites.

It is a great honor for a district to be chosen. Likewise it is an honor to be a member of the families chosen to do the actual planting, tending, and harvesting of the crop for the Great Festival. Once the actual fields have been selected, a small shrine is built at each field called the *Hasshin Den* or *Yashin Den,* meaning "Hall of the Eight Kami." Just why these eight are chosen is not known, though it is possible that in early times these were the *kami* who protected agriculture.

After the selection of the fields, there are various ceremonies that are performed from time to time. When the rice is ripe, in the middle of September occurs the ceremony of Plucking the Grain Heads. First occurs the purification ceremony at the river for all the men and women involved in the harvesting ceremony and the Imperial Commissioner. After the purification ceremony, the impurities of the individuals are cast into the river with the tossing of the pieces of the sakaki branches onto the flowing water. On the following morning the actual harvesting begins. Formerly the plants were pulled up by the roots and each stalk plucked separately. In the last ceremony, the one for the present emperor, sickles were used. Four bunches of rice are first gathered and these are placed on a small table in a small shrine just to the north of the Shrine of the Eight Kami. This small shrine has no *kami*-seat because the *kami* of this shrine is the rice, or rice spirit, itself. It is the rice of these first four bunches which is used in the communion meal between the emperor and the *kami.* The remainder of the rice in the field, harvested by modern methods, is used for making white and black *sake* which is part of the later ceremony. This *sake* is brewed within the precincts of the Kamo Shrine in Kyoto.

On the night before the Great Festival, there occurs the Soul Pacification Ceremony.* The purpose of this is to tranquilize the soul of the emperor and lengthen his life. It includes ancient magical practices along with some awareness of the importance of unifying all of the psychological forces at work in the human personality. It is based on the ancient Japanese psychology of the "four spirits" in man—a gentle spirit, a rough spirit, a luck spirit, and a wondrous spirit. All these spirits must be harmonized and none should be allowed to wander from the body.

---

* *Chinkon-sai,* in so-called Chinese sounds; *Mi-tama-shizume-no-matsuri,* in Japanese sounds.

O-taue-sai. The rice-planting ceremony at Kirishima Jingū, in a special place provided inside the sacred garden. (Kyūshū region.)

Onbashira-sai. The sacred poles which once in seven years are raised in the four corners of the shrine grounds are being drawn down from the sacred forest at Suwa Taisha. In very early Shinto, the *kami* was closely associated with trees. (Chūbu region.)

The ceremony first invites nine *kami* to descend to the sacred place. Eight of them descend on one sacred branch (*himorogi*) and the other one, the *kami* who sets things straight, Ō-Naobi-no-Kami, rests on the second sacred branch. While dance and music are performed, eight sacred treasures are placed in front of these *kami*. These treasures represent the treasures given to Ninigi-no-mikoto when he came down from heaven, and were magical de-vices used for protecting and prolonging life. Two boxes are brought in, one containing clothing belonging to the emperor and the other containing a cord of thick white silk. A female ritualist with bells in one hand and a spear in the other mounts an object which looks like an inverted tub. Striking the tub or drum with the spear, she counts to ten, and at each count a knot is tied in the silk cord, which represents the emperor's life-cord. The chief ritualist then shakes the box of the emperor's clothing ten times in front of the *kami*. The boxes are then carried out.

The dance on the inverted tub has its prototype in the mythi-cal account of the dancing in front of the heavenly cave where Amaterasu had hidden herself. So says the *Kogoshūi*, written in the Heian period. The shaking of the treasures and the emperor's clothing is a part of the ancient magic thought of as prolonging the emperor's life or protecting him from illness. There is nothing in the myth about tying the thread. This very possibly means ty-ing together the souls of the emperor as a part of the harmonizing process.[6] On the following evening the emperor performs the Great New Food Festival. Let us briefly note the setting for this occasion.

The Yuki Den, the Suki Den and the fence which surrounds them all reflect Japan's ancient past. The fence is constructed of simple brushwood, decorated with boughs of the pasania on which are hung white streamers. There is a gateway in *torii* style on each side of the enclosure, constructed of wood from which the bark has not been removed. There is also a brushwood fence between the Yuki Den and the Suki Den with a gate in the middle. The two halls themselves, exact duplicates, stand on piles and repro-duce the primitive Japanese dwelling with the cross-beams of the roof-ends projecting beyond the ridges. (Aspects of the architec-

Hi-no-mai-matsuri. Celebrated on February 7. Here, fire is being kindled according to ancient rites. (Chūbu region.)

Mi-taue Shinko-shiki. A ceremony of planting the rice paddies, celebrated July 28 at Aso Jinja. (Kyūshū region.)

ture, which recall Polynesian-type structures, have been preserved in some of the Shinto shrines.) The bark is not removed from any of the timbers used in the buildings. The roofs are of miscanthus thatch while the walls and ceilings are of matting. The veranda of each building is of bamboo covered with rush matting. Each ritual hall is divided into an inner room and an outer room, with a red screen bordered with white paper hanging between.

The tools and furnishings which are placed in these rooms reflect the life of very ancient Japan. Prior to the modern period scholars who tried to publish what they knew about these sacred items were sometimes put into prison. The most important item in the inner chamber is the kami-seat, or *shinza*. Holtom describes it as follows:

> It is a great couch made of large rectangular slabs of pressed straw (*tatami*). It is set with head to the south and foot to the north. For the foundation of the couch six *tatami* are placed end to end, thus providing a base three feet wide and twelve feet long. Above this are laid two *tatami* three feet wide and nine feet long, so placed as to overlap the foundation *tatami* by a foot or more, thus providing a broad shelf extending along the entire eastern side of the couch. On top of these, in position corresponding to the lowest tier, are laid two *tatami* nine feet in length. The height of the couch is brought to approximately that of an ordinary bed. At the head is placed a peculiar pillow of triangular shape, known as the *saka makura*, the "hill-pillow." Over the uppermost *tatami* and pillow are spread, one above the other eight successive layers of reed matting. . . . Completely covering the eight-fold matting is spread a cloth of pure white raw silk. At the head of the couch above the pillow is folded a simple unlined garment of white silk."[7]

Nearby are placed a fan, a comb, and a pair of slippers.

This couch is a witness to the food festival which takes place near it. What and whom the couch represents is not written down anywhere. The most probable explanation is that the couch is for the emperor who has just died but whose soul is thought of as being present as his successor goes through the sacred rites of the Great New Food Festival. Others have suggested it is where

Amaterasu reclines, though when the emperor serves her food, he does so just to the east of the *kami*-seat where a Food-Mat of the Kami is spread next to the emperor's food-mat. In carrying out the food ritual, his mat is so placed that he is facing in the direction of Ise Shrine. At the foot of the *kami*-seat, placed on small tables, are the garments for the *kami*, one table with garments which are soft and the other with garments that are rough.

In the evening the lamps in the Yuki Den and Suki Den are lit by the process of rubbing two pieces of wood together. The emperor leaves the palace and proceeds to the special building for the ceremonial purification. Then he puts on ceremonial robes of pure white silk. Court musicians begin to play the "Song of the Pounding of the Rice" and maidens go through the motions of placing the rice in mortars and pounding it with pestles. In modern times the actual hulling and polishing is done at the place of gathering the rice, but the old ritual is still adhered to on the night of the offering of the new food. The chief Shinto ritualist then reads a prayer in the outer hall of the Yuki Den and awaits the imperial procession. While the court musicians sing the folk songs native to the Yuki district, the emperor moves into the outer hall of the Yuki Den. The procession of the sacred food offerings begins from the cookhouse. A colorful line of ritualists and imperial female attendants slowly bring all the items used in the food ceremony. Over two dozen people make up the procession. When the head of the procession reaches the Yuki Den, the emperor passes into the inner chamber. Only two ritualists are allowed to enter that room, both of them female attendants.

The food for the *kami* is brought in first and placed on the food-mat of the *kami*. Then the offerings of *sake* are made. At the conclusion of the offerings, the emperor claps his hands three times. Then the emperor is served his own meal and *sake*. When the communion meal is over, all utensils and offerings are removed in the same fashion as they were presented. There is a handwashing ceremony, then the emperor withdraws and there is a general recessional. This ritual in the Yuki Den ends shortly before midnight. At 2:00 a.m. the same ritual is repeated in the Suki Den.

Offering of Seventy-five Dishes. At the annual festival at Kibitsu Jinja, seventy-five dishes of food offerings are presented to the *kami*. Performed on May 13 and October 19. (Chūgoku region.)

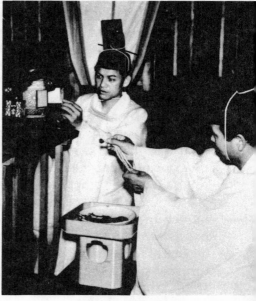

Festival praying for grain. Lighting the sacred fire using a fllintstone at Takase Jinja in early June. (Chūbu region.)

What is the meaning of this Shinto festival with its ancient undertones? Feelings have been incorporated in these ceremonies which the Japanese have never really tried to put into words. In 1928, when the present emperor repeated these ancient forms, Japanese writers wrote explanations for the general public which were in almost every case much too simple or superficial. To say as was then said, that the emperor is simply giving thanks to the *kami,* is not to say enough. For many things which may not make much sense when presented in a rationalistic fashion are at work in this complex ceremony.

For one thing, the *kami* are being informed that a new emperor has succeeded to the Japanese throne. The soul of the emperor who has died is being sped on its way, and a new emperor seeks communion with the *kami,* especially with Amaterasu, the ancestral *kami.* Some scholars insist that in this ritual when the emperor is alone with the *kami,* a new emperor is being "born." This is his "rebirth" experience.

The offering of the new food would certainly seem to be an expression of thanksgiving to the *kami.* But the elaborate care put into the choosing of the rice fields, the sowing of the grain, the tending, and the harvesting, would suggest also something of the concern with which the ancient Japanese sought to protect the food supply by staying in harmony with the powers of growth and fertility. As with all religions, magical attitudes and profound religious attitudes intermingle in these rituals with their elaborate details. That much of the ritual may have had only psychological, rather than scientific, value does not minimize its significance in the slightest as expressions of Japanese man's concern to remain in harmony with the world of the *kami.* The ancient *Dai-jō-sai* may well have been an attempt to get magical power for the new emperor. But more than that, it probably symbolized a literal union between the mind of the *kami* and the mind of the emperor. In Oriental society generally, to eat together meant to become a member of that group, an intimate member. By eating the same food with *kami,* whether the main *kami* in the ceremony was a goddess of food or Amaterasu, the emperor belonged to the *kami;* he was accepted as having the same qualities as the *kami.* In other words, he became *kami.*

Communion meals the world around have been given various interpretations by theologians of different groups. But back of all communion meals must lie some human grasping after a more-than-rational union with the forces of the cosmos. For the Japanese people traditionally, *Dai-jō-sai* has meant that their emperor in some deep sense became *kami*. Before that intimate communion could take place, there were elaborate preparations so that the rice might be pure. The emperor also went through many purifications in order that he might be pure.

Here lies the root of the idea which was distorted by the Japanese military leaders in the twentieth century, namely, that the emperor is a "living *kami*," or *kami* incarnate. The emperor's mind-heart (*kokoro*) is the mind-heart of *kami*. That the Japanese people—soldiers and civilians alike—gave up the intention to resist the allied invasion of Japan to the last man in a desperate holocaust that would have cost both the Americans and the Japanese hundreds of thousands of lives, is essentially traceable to one man and the strange power he had over the minds of his subjects—namely, the emperor. By taking the reins of government momentarily into his own hands in an unprecedented way, as he did on two crucial occasions when the Japanese cabinet was badly split on the question of whether to accept the Allied terms for surrender, he got the Japanese to do by one radio broadcast what no other person or group of persons could have done. It is no exaggeration to say that this was because the underlying Shinto feeling still present, at least in the subconscious if not the conscious minds of millions of his subjects, was able to respond to the emperor's appeal. Only a tiny handful of the armed forces made any effort to resist the appeal to lay down arms, and yet Japan still had a million soldiers in the islands. Months of tough guerrilla warfare could have been carried out in the mountainous areas of the islands. For the historians, either Japanese or American, to overlook the operation of this non-logical factor, is to place too much emphasis on political, economic, and military categories of interpretation. What the agnostic or intellectual buries is often only dead for the intellectual who tends to forget how much of life still eludes quantitative methods of measurement.

CHAPTER SIX

Purification in Shinto

We slowly mounted the flight of steps that led to the sanctuary of Amaterasu-Ōmikami. We had walked beneath cryptomeria trees which were centuries old, trees beneath which millions of pilgrims had walked on their way to the Grand Shrine of Ise. At the top of the stone steps we turned to the left and my Japanese friend introduced me to a priest standing there. We were to be allowed to go inside the fenced area where most worshippers never enter. Only the emperor, members of his family, and a few others are allowed to approach closely to the shrine containing the sacred mirror which, according to legend, was given to Amaterasu's divine grandson when he descended to earth to rule the islands of Japan.

Before we were permitted to enter this sacred area, we bowed before the priest as he sprinkled salt over us. As we bowed low a second time, the priest purified us with the ō-nusa, a short stick with white cut-papers hanging from it. Then he opened the inner gate and we followed him across the inner courtyard, walking on the carefully placed boulders which constituted the ground-covering. Directly in front of the sanctuary we knelt and offered our silent respect before the sacred mirror which is never open to human gaze.

Purification rites are very ancient in Shinto. All developed religions have some ritual actions which relate to man's desire to be purified or cleansed. Modern man's growing knowledge of the deeper aspects of the human consciousness suggests that the cleanliness which is sought is more metaphysical than physical. Lustrations; baptisms; bathing in temple tanks, rivers, or the sea —each has a more religious than hygienic significance. To under-

stand Shinto it is necessary to understand the Japanese feeling
for purification.

The mythical basis for purification in Shinto is found in the
story of Izanagi purifying himself at a river-mouth where the
waters emptied into the sea. He had been to the underworld and
had contacted death. In Shinto death is pollution, though death
has never been regarded as a punishment for sin. Although
Izanagi and Izanami are separated by death, which is symbolized
by the rock barrier between the underworld and the ordinary
world, the alienation between male and female is not a radical
alienation. The Earth Mother, Izanami, is left behind, but nature
as such does not become a threat to man. Izanagi, through the
ritual of purification, returns to his former role of creating. He
begins immediately to give birth to other *kami*. This suggests
something very important about the Shinto interpretation of human experience. The growth process or man's creative activity
may be temporarily blocked or thwarted, but it is never perman-
ently distorted, nor is it poisoned at its very root. The ethical implications of this will be discussed in the following chapter.

In the Shinto myth, whenever there is violence on the part
of any *kami*, the result is further productivity. This is illustrated
not only in the account of Izanagi's slaying of the Fire Kami (who
had caused the death of Izanami), but also in the account of the
Moon Kami's slaying of the Food Kami. Oxen, the horse, millet,
the silk-worm, rice, and beans are all produced from the dismem-
bered pieces of the Food Kami.[1]

In very ancient times the pollutions from which man suffered were such things as disease, blood associated with menstru-
ation and childbirth, wounds, and death. Various rites of a magical nature were prescribed in order to gain release from these.
Some of the practices, in addition to their psychological value,
very probably had concrete survival-value, such as the use of salt
water or salt. The long-standing popularity of the Japanese bath
is traceable to the ancient Japanese use of water for purification.

In early Japan there were other actions which resulted in
pollution in addition to those just mentioned. The *Engishiki*,
completed in 927 A.D., contains twenty-seven ancient prayers

called *norito*. These tell us quite a bit about the early Japanese religion. One of these prayers, called the Great Exorcism of the Last Day of the Sixth Month, lists "heavenly sins" and "earthly sins." Under the former heading come breaking down the ridges between fields, covering up the ditches, releasing the irrigation sluices, double planting, setting up stakes, skinning alive, skinning backwards, and defecation. All of these suggest the misdeeds committed in heaven by Susanoo, the impetuous brother of Amaterasu. It has been suggested that several of these "heavenly sins," including that of causing ritual impurity by defecation, were related to early black magic practices.[2]

The "earthly sins" enumerated in this *norito* are cutting living flesh, cutting dead flesh, white leprosy, skin excrescences, violating one's own mother or child, violating a mother and her child, transgression with animals, woes from creeping insects, from the birds on high, killing animals, and witchcraft. Any one of these actions results in pollution.

When translators use the English word "sin" for the Japanese term *tsumi*, persons brought up in contact with the Jewish or Christian concept of sin are apt to be misled. Sin in Christianity is tied in with the *sin of origin*, and this involves a very specific idea of violating the "will of God." This idea of original sin or violating a command of a transcendent deity is absent in Shinto. Hence, when "heavenly" or "earthly" sins are referred to, it might be better to use the word "offense" or "defilement." Westerners with a Semitic background will be led astray less.

The same prayer referred to above goes on to say that where such offenses have taken place, the priestly family of the Nakatomi are to prepare myriad strips of sedge reeds, many narrow pieces of wood, to be placed on thousands of tables, and proceed to recite the heavenly ritual so that the *kami* will hear and receive the words.

When they thus hear and receive,
Then, beginning with the court of the Sovereign Grandchild,
  In the lands of the four quarters under the heavens,
    Each and every sin will be gone.

As the gusty wind blows apart the myriad leaves of heavenly clouds;
   As the morning mist, the evening mist is blown away by the
      morning wind, the evening wind;
As the large ship anchored in the spacious port is untied at the
      prow and untied at the stern
    And pushed out into the great ocean;
As the luxuriant clump of trees on yonder hill
  Is cut away at the base with a tempered sickle, a sharp sickle—
As a result of the exorcism of the purification,
   There will be no sins left.
They will be taken into the great ocean
  By the goddess called Seoritsu-hime,
  Who dwells in the rapids of the rapid-running rivers
    Which fall surging perpendicular
    From the summits of the high mountains and the summits of
    the low mountains.
When she thus takes them,
  They will be swallowed with a gulp
    By the goddess called Haya-akitsu-hime,
    Who dwells in the wild brine, the myriad currents of
    the brine.
    In the myriad meeting-places of the brine of
    the many briny currents.
When she thus swallows them with a gulp,
  The deity called Ibukido-nushi,
    Who dwells in the Ibuki-do,
  Will blow them away with his breath to the land of Hades,
    the under-world.
When he thus blows them away,
  The deity called Haya-sasura-hime,
    Who dwells in the land of Hades, the under-world,
  Will wander off with them and lose them.

              .   .   .

Each and every sin will be gone.[3]

This prayer of the Great Exorcism certainly includes a feeling for the ethical as well as the psychological dimension in hu-

Tsuina ceremony. On the Setsubun festival in February, an exorcism ceremony is performed before the shrine, Nagata Jinja. (Kinki region.)

Hamaori-sai. A purification ceremony in which the *kami* is taken in procession to the seashore about eight miles away from the shrine early in the morning. Performed on July 15 at Samukawa Jinja. (Kantō region.)

man life. But there is no philosophizing in the prayer itself. As
the centuries passed, persons appeared who put into words the
distinction between outer purity and inner purity. Ichijō Kaneyo-
shi wrote in the fifteenth century: "There are two significations
of purity in Shinto: one is outer purity (bodily purity) and the
other inner purity (purity of heart). If a man is truly sincere in
mind he will be sure to succeed in realizing a communion with
the Divine. This is no other than inner purity or sincerity, which
means purity of heart or uprightness of heart."[4]

In the *Shinto Gobusho* it is written: "To do good is to be pure;
to commit evil is to be impure. The deities dislike evil deeds, because they are impure."[5] A man named Saka Shibutsu kept a
diary of his pilgrimage to the Ise Shrine in 1342. He wrote:

> It is quite customary for us neither to bring any offerings to the
> Goddess nor to carry rosaries about us like Buddhists. In short, we
> have nothing special wherewith to recommend ourselves in petition-
> ing her Divinity. This is the true signification of inner purity. Wash-
> ing oneself in the sea water, and being cleansed of the bodily filth—
> this is outer purity. Being pure in mind and body, our soul is at one
> with the Divine, and divinity in humanity thus realized, there re-
> mains no desire unsatisfied—there is no occasion for further petition
> or prayer to the Goddess. This is the true esoteric meaning of wor-
> shipping the Sun Goddess at the Ise Shrine. Being thus enlightened
> by the Shinto priest of the shrine, I was overwhelmed with a sense
> of pious joy, and burst into tears of gratitude.[6]

This distinction between inner and outer purity is of course a
development of sophisticated thought. If early Japanese man made
no such distinction, that is not necessarily a sign of his lack of
capacity for a whole-natured response.

In Shinto, the purification rites have always been a preparation either for communing with *kami* or for returning to everyday
life. In ancient times purification was often used to prevent sickness or to get rid of illness. In modern times, there are people
who go to a shrine after an illness, for purification. This undoubtedly has beneficial psychological aspects in many cases. In
earlier periods, bathing in the sea was a common form of purifica-

tion. This was usually done after a funeral, for example. In some villages in modern Japan, after a funeral the people wade into the sea up to their knees. Other modern Japanese sprinkle salt over themselves before entering their homes after attending a funeral service. These are simplified versions of the older method of immersing the entire body in the sea after a funeral. All of them are preparations for a return to normal life.

THE WAY OF DISCIPLINES AND MUMMIFICATION

Influences from outside the main stream of Shinto, coming mostly from Taoism and Buddhism and possibly encouraged by Folk Shinto beliefs, were to introduce another element into the Shinto concept of purification, at times making it resemble the asceticism of India. Having heard of these ascetic practices, we decided to visit several shrines and mountain retreats that had felt this influence. This took us to some Buddhist centers and brought us into contact with the practices of the mountain-worshippers or strolling monks known as *yamabushi*.

In front of us was a mummified figure wearing a pointed hat and the colored robes of a Buddhist monk. The dark skin was pulled tightly over the facial bones, the eyes were gone, and only the sockets peered at us. Several teeth stood out quite prominently in the mouth; the skin was pulled taut over hands and arms and fingers. Asceticism such as can be found in Hinduism, Buddhism, and Christianity cannot be found in Shinto proper. Yet ascetic practices did creep into some Shinto places of worship in the form of *shugen-dō*, the "way of disciplines." This mummy at whom we were gazing was a product of this mountaineering asceticism. With persons like him, what had been only a *means* in Shinto apparently had become an *end*. What in Shinto was only a preparation for communing with *kami* became under alien influences an effort to become *kami* or a Buddha-in-a-body.

These ascetics liked to practice their disciplines in the mountains. At some places the mountain itself was worshipped as the *kami*. Often these mountain-worshippers would find a spot in a Shinto shrine or in the precincts of a Shingon or Tendai Buddhist temple. Sometimes they would even build a shrine for themselves. A few of them chose to spend years preparing their bodies for mummification so they could be worshipped as gods.[7]

Shugen-dō, the way of disciplines, seems to have been a Japanese phenomenon originally, associated with mountain worship. However, Taoist influence from the magical side, not the philosophical side, seems to have come into it. This combined with some of the shamanistic elements in folk religion in Japan. However, it was Shingon Buddhism which was to influence those practicing extreme disciplines to think of becoming mummies. For it was this school of Buddhism which had a doctrine concerning becoming a Buddha in one's own body. According to tradition, Kōbō Daishi had become a Buddha in his own body in a cave on Mount Kōya.

An important center of mountain asceticism was Mount Yudono in Yamagata prefecture. Hence we decided to make a pilgrimage to the holy place up on the mountainside where a hot spring bubbles out over a huge round rock. On the particular day we made the trip up the trail, any modern *yamabushi* would have had difficulty making the ascent in peace. A long line of from five hundred to six hundred high school students, all in uniforms, were ascending the trail at a lively pace. In groups of fifty or sixty at a time, they removed their shoes and socks at the shrine and were admitted by a Shinto priest to the inner precincts where they could stand or climb on the rock over which the hot water poured. We were told that the distance from the starting point was less than two kilometers, but the trail was often rough and steep and it seemed several times that. It was an October day with the sun shining brightly, and on all sides were the beautiful Japanese maples in their brilliant colors. We stopped at several open-air shrines along the way to catch our breath, remembering that when the ascetics had climbed the path, they had stopped at each of thirty small shrines on their way up. Also, they had made the climb three times a day.

We retraced our steps down the trail ahead of the students, and decided to seek an interview with the eighty-year-old monk who used to be in charge of Chūren-ji, the most important temple of the Yudono sect of *shugen-dō* where the training was carried on. We found him at Ryūkaku-ji and we talked for some time about the training preparatory to self-mummification. He described in detail the rigorous disciplines of the ascetics. For one thousand days they abstained from five kinds of grain, including rice and wheat. This practice was related to the legend that Kōbō Daishi gave an injunction near the end of his life, that abstaining from cereals had been a part of his daily practice after the twelfth day of the eleventh month of the year 832.

During this time of abstinence from five cereals, the ascetics climbed to the shrine on Yudono Mountain three times a day. They secluded themselves at a place called the Swamp of Wizards. The length of time that they abstained from cereals varied from less than three years to eight years. Their diet consisted largely of nuts, pine bark, and grass roots. Whereas the first thousand days of abstention involved the repudiation of only five types of cereal, the remainder of the period seems to have involved abstention from ten kinds of cereal. A diet of nuts and roots only was considered best for preparing their bodies to become mummified. Of the various ascetics who underwent the long disciplines at Mount Yudono, the priest said, the one whose body was most ready for mummification was the man who kept up his disciplines for four thousand days.

The mummy enshrined at Honmyō-ji in Higashi-Iwamoto entered a stone chamber under the ground in 1683 and died there while chanting. His body was dried with a charcoal fire and incense fumes. Then it was buried again for about three years and when it was removed, it had become completely mummified.[8]

In the case of the latest mummified ascetic, 1868 or 1881, the old priest told us he had spent only one thousand days in his disciplines since he became too weak to continue further. Thus his body was much harder to mummify after his death. The body cavity had been filled with lime powder up to the neck, but this is the only case of a special operation being carried out. We were allowed to examine this mummy closely at Nangaku-ji and the priest was willing for photographs to be taken.

But let us return again to the mummification preparations. After the ascetic decided that he had had enough of the discipline, he would return to his own temple and wait for his death. When he or his associates thought that death was not more than ten days away, the ascetic would enter a small box, about one meter square, and sit in the *zazen* position, that is, with legs folded. A hole was then dug in the ground four meters deep, and the box with the ascetic inside was lowered into it and covered with earth. Three or four bamboo poles were stuck into the box to provide air. The man in the box had a small bell which he rang while chanting. In each case the bell was heard less than a week, the priest told us. Either the original estimate of the nearness of death was quite accurate or life in the box was not worth much more than a few days at best.

After the bell was no longer heard by the persons above ground, the box was dug up and the body taken out. A board was tied along the line of the backbone to keep the body upright in the *zazen* position. The mummy at Kaikō-ji in Sakata City shows the marks of the rope on its body. The body was then put into another box, of pine or chestnut. The ashes of rice husks were put into cotton bags and packed around the body. Then the box was buried for three years. At the end of that time the box was dug up and the body was taken out and put into a building called *Rokkaudō* (Six-Corner Building). In this building more than twenty sticks of candles were burnt, each candle weighing two pounds. Mugwort leaves were also burnt. How long it took to dry out the bodies is not known now. However, all of them were dried out at Chūren-ji, the priest said.

In the case of those ascetics who wanted to become "Buddhas in the body," it is quite apparent that they had little in common with Shinto. Shingon Buddhism provided for them a philosophical basis for their practices, but ego needs must have been at work also. These men aspired to become objects of worship after their death. Since they were not married, they had no children who

Mummy of mountain ascetic (Buddhist) in Tsuruoka City. (Tōhoku region.)

Stopping-place for worship for mountain ascetics on Mt. Yudono. (Tōhoku region.)

would remember them faithfully before the family altar. By becoming mummies, this need could be satisfied as well as their own religious needs. It is an interesting fact, according to the former head of Chūren-ji, that no Buddhist monk ever sought to mummify himself. Indeed, most of the monks despised these ascetics who had no interest in study. To some extent the matter of status was involved here. Professional Buddhist monks wore colored clothing. Five colors were used to show respective ranking. The non-professional ascetic, however, could wear only white, a color never used by the professional monks. However, once these ascetics were made into mummies, colored clothing of the highest rank could be placed upon their mummified bodies by other ascetics and by the numerous believers. In this way they not only achieved the desired status in this world after their demise, but they also became Buddhas.

In this same district where we visited the place for *shugen-dō* training and the Buddhist temples where three of the mummies are kept, the story is told of a fairly young ascetic who was practising his disciplines very strictly in the mountains. The young woman whom he had been supposed to marry sought him out in his mountain retreat, pleading with him to return to ordinary life. When he could not dissuade her through words alone, the monk went back into the cave and came out shortly to hand her something wrapped up. Opening it she discovered it was his penis. It is possible that this is not entirely legend. The Waseda University team of scholars which carefully examined the mummies reported that one of them was found to have no penis.

The asceticism carried to such extremes by these persons has nothing in common with the Shinto acceptance of the body as sound or good. That desperate efforts to become a Buddha are also contrary to many of the teachings of the schools of Buddhism also goes without saying. But these men were seeking a kind of "individual salvation" that has no place in the Shinto tradition. The way of disciplines reflects much more of an individualistic orientation than Shinto. The great prayers of Shinto ritual have to do with the food supply, thanksgiving for good harvest, and protection from wind, flood, and fire. These prayers are all oriented toward the group, not the individual.

On the contrary, these mountain ascetics made a business out of their individual-oriented practices. They promised recovery from illness, escape from bad luck, special favors—all for a fee, of course. In many cases they played upon the superstitious fears of the peasants. They also organized groups which they themselves led to various mountain shrines and temples. It was a mixture of folk religion, magical practices, Buddhist philosophy, and Shinto, in varying degrees.

Under today's law, self-mummification is hardly practical, as the laws forbid opening up one's grave. However, *shugen-dō*, the way of asceticism, is not dead. Although thousands of Japanese now climb the mountains only as a form of recreation or sightseeing, others still prefer to follow some of the disciplines of the *yamabushi*, the mountaineering ascetics. At one Shinto shrine the priest said that the practice of asceticism was now open to women also in his district. But if Shinto is true to its own tradition, such disciplines will never become an end in themselves. Like purification rituals, they should be only a preparation for returning to one's true nature if it has been lost in the confusion of modern living.

Shinto accepts the relativity of life but does not lament its transitoriness as Buddhism does. Accepting relativity, it does not seek an absolute Heaven or Pure Land. It accepts the beauty of nature but does not leave nature untouched. Rather it seeks to transform nature through aesthetic appreciation. Shinto accepts the desires of the human organism as good, but it does not revere them to the point of sensuality, for where the good of the group clashes with individual desires, it is the individual desires that are relinquished. Religions with a taste for the absolute may find this attitude hard to understand, but it is there just the same.

CHAPTER SEVEN

Ethics in Shinto

Contrary to the opinions of some Western writers on Shinto, there are ethical teachings in the Shinto tradition. The ethic can be called a *situational* ethic. That is, there is no one way of doing the right thing, unvarying from age to age. In each situation the answer must be earnestly sought and then put into practice. This can be called a *contextual* approach since the context plays such an important part in the decision. The Shinto ethic can also be called an ethic of *intention* in that great stress is put on the motivation, the inner springs of action. The heart-mind must be right. One must have meditated upon his proposed action seriously, undergoing purification and then approaching *kami*. Then one can perform the action.

Thus Shinto ethics are relative. There is no absolute word handed down from a transcendent source of authority. There is nothing resembling the Law of Moses or the Code of Manu. The word Shinto means "the way of the *kami*," but man is capable of walking that way. He is not called to an impossible task. The basic attitude toward life is expressed by the word *makoto*. *Makoto* is common both to *kami* and to men. The term is usually translated as honesty, conscientiousness, or truthfulness. However, if these are taken in a narrowly ethical sense, something of the Shinto flavor is lost. There is a dynamic, psychological dimension that is very important. He who practices *makoto* is "true" to the total situation. He is in harmony with *kami* and is doing his very best under the circumstances. "Truth" here is not an abstract something but a concrete living-out of the present situation. The search for Truth in the Western philosophical sense of an "Ultimate Truth" is foreign to the life of Shinto. Many Japanese call this attitude a purely Western one. Truth in the sense of *makoto* involves an inner searching of the heart which is just as important as the outer confronting of the situation.

When a man is "untrue" to the situation and does that which is harmful to himself or to others, it is not because there is some source of evil in himself. It is because of lack of proper awareness. In early Shinto no evil was thought of as originating internally. Evil always arose under external influence. Purification was to remove this external influence producing evil. This holds true also of what is called "moral evil." Professor Sokyō Ono of the Shinto university wrote recently:

> Moral evil must also be expressed passively as the result of having been deprived of normal moral consciousness and having been caused to do evil; like disaster or pollution, moral evil is also counted as an affliction suffered passively. Here, that which judges between good and evil and determines the standards of good and evil is the soul. The soul distinguishes between good and evil together with the gods, or according to their will. The ultimately correct judgment is the judgment made in the condition of human-divine unity. However, this judgment is not one fixed as a universal law. The good or evil of an action, the meaning and value of an action differs according to the motive, the object, the time, place, and relationship. Concrete actions differ in value each time performed according to the concrete circumstances.[1]

When we consider some of the modern theories and practices regarding anti-social behavior, the result of the work of psychotherapists and educators, we cannot dismiss the Shinto attitude toward the source of evil as primitive or quasi-magical, as some past writers have done. If man is fundamentally sound or healthy in essence (as some Western schools of thought and not just Shinto thinkers are willing to assume), evil is more a distortion or the result of bad interpersonal environmental conditions than a corruption of the heart or the will. Metaphysical assumptions lurk in every psychological as well as theological statement, of course. But it can make a real difference in the actual handling of human life-situations whether one is thinking in terms of a cosmic source of evil which is a fatal infection in man's nature, or in terms of a cosmos which is fundamentally "healthy" at core. To think of the cosmos as at war with itself—God versus Satan—is quite different from thinking of the cosmos as essentially harmonized with itself.

Traditionally, Shinto has spoken for the undivided cosmos. This is quite clear. Though Shinto affirms a plurality of *kami*, it has always believed in their harmonious cooperation. Popular Christian thought, affirming a monotheism in theory, has postulated a divided universe with Satan able to defeat the power and purpose of God so far as the destiny of many individual souls is concerned, even though God is declared to be omnipotent. On all metaphysical issues there is no decision capable of proof or disproof. One always chooses on the basis of incomplete evidence. Shinto chooses the unity of the cosmos and affirms the reality of continuing growth, creativity, and capacity for harmonious development.

LIMITATIONS OF ETHICAL CATEGORIES

The West has been strongly inclined to use ethical terms when speaking of religious and metaphysical matters such as the nature of man or the nature of God. Shinto is less inclined to do this, though Motoori Norinaga sometimes wrote about the *kami* as though they could be divided into "good" *kami* and "bad" *kami*. The Shinto myth describes how Izanagi purified himself after his return from the realm of death. At that time Izanagi gave birth to Magatsubi-no-kami. This name has sometimes been translated as "Kami of Great Evils." Many scholars connected this with Motoori's theory that one kind of *kami* excels in goodness and another kind excels in badness. This idea came from popular Chinese Taoism and from some of the later followers of Confucius. However, there is no such thing as a "*kami* of goodness" in Shinto, though there are *kami* who seek to make things good. Nor is there such a thing as a "*kami* of badness" in Shinto, though there are *kami* who are violent, rough, and fierce. Also, each *kami* has its "rough side" (*ara-mi-tama*) just as it has its "gentle side" (*nigi-mi-tama*).

Hirata Atsutane's treatment of the above-mentioned passage in the myth of Izanagi's purification is much more thorough than that of Motoori. He points out that Magatsubi-no-kami is the *kami* who hates pollution, being born at the time that Izanagi was concentrating his thoughts on cleansing himself from the pollution of death. He adds that Magatsubi-no-kami becomes violent and rough when there are pollutions and wrong things.[2]

The term *magaru* (which occurs in the *kami's* name) can mean "to bend," "to be awry," or "to be perverse." In the above myth, no sooner has Izanagi given birth to Magatsubi-no-kami than he gives birth to Naobi-no-kami. The term *nao* is related to the word which means to be mended, to be set right, to be rectified (*naoru*). In other words, there are elements in nature which can only be described as distorting or perverting. But in conjunction with these are elements that make straight the distorted; correct the out-of-line. Motoori, like many other Japanese scholars who wanted to go back to the Japanese sources, was unable to shake off much of the Chinese influence in his own attitudes. There is no basis in the Shinto myth for his concept of "bad *kami*." What he called "bad *kami*" should have been called rough *kami* or distorting *kami*. Except when under foreign influences, Shinto has never been prone to use ethical terms for describing either religious experience or the *kami* mentioned in the myths. This seems to reflect the feeling that terms which may be relevant for the laws or customs of society are inappropriate when used to describe either the universe or human nature. In other words, ethical categories which have been so important in the thinking of Western theologians, have never been given primacy in Shinto circles. This means that modern Shinto should have no special difficulty in coming to terms with the findings of modern depth psychology as it seeks to understand the dynamics of human behavior without applying rigid ethical yardsticks.

SHINTO IDEAS OF THE SOUL

A discussion of ethics in Shinto has to take into account Shinto ideas of the soul and of human nature in general. Very little is said in the early Shinto records about man's soul. *Tama*, which meant a beautiful jewel or mysterious rock, also meant spirit or soul, especially a pure, lofty soul. The terms *mono* and *mi* also meant spirit but apparently a spirit of a lower order or quality. *Mono* seems to have meant the spirits of animals, whereas *tama* was a divine or semi-divine spirit.* *Tamashii* is also used for spirit or soul. Anesaki suggests that this probably meant originally "ball-wind." If so, this would correlate it with the ancient words for soul in other languages, suggesting wind, air, or breath.[3]

The Japanese word *kokoro*, which means both mind and heart, is used synonymously in some of the Japanese classical books with the word for belly, *hara*. The old Japanese phrase still heard in certain polite expressions today, *mi-kage* (august shadow), meant august soul, *mi-tama*. To refer to the august shadow came to stand for the grace of *kami* or the grace of Buddha. The mirror also seems to have stood for the soul or spirit in ancient times. The grandson of Amaterasu was told to look into the divine mirror which she had given him, in order to see her divine self.[4]

In ancient Shinto, as at present, there were rituals for calming or pacifying the soul of the living person, in addition to rituals for pacifying the souls of the dead. In the *Manyōshū* the poet speaks of Empress Jingū's pacifying her *kokoro*, meaning her belly (*hara*). Here the reference is to the empress's device of binding a couple of stones endowed with magical virtue around the lower part of her body so she would not give birth to her child while on her military expedition against Korea. The words here thus would seem to refer to the quieting of her womb.[5]

We have already referred to the concept of the four spirits—the spirit empowered to rule with authority (*ara-mi-tama*),

---

* In present-day Japanese, *mono* is used to mean object, being, or thing. *Mi* now means body, also fruit. Thus it is very difficult to know what *mono* and *mi* meant in the early period.

thought of as vigorous and rough; the spirit empowered to lead to harmony or union, thought of as remaining always with the body (*nigi-mi-tama*); the spirit causing mysterious transformations (*kushi-mi-tama*); the spirit imparting blessings (*saki-mi-tama*). Japanese scholars of different periods have not agreed as to the meaning of these four spirits, but the early Japanese seem to have believed that each individual has several kinds of souls.[6]

It is quite clear that the ancient Japanese thought their souls could leave their bodies temporarily, for the ritual for pacifying souls was a very important one. This festival took place before the important ritual of offering the first harvest to the *kami*. From the legendary period all the way down to the present emperor, the sovereign of Japan has always gone through this soul-pacifying ceremony before offering the new harvest. This ritual for pacifying the soul, with its apparently magical features, was a kind of ritual psychotherapy to keep the "rough soul" from wandering off at will in any direction.[7]

When one raises the question as to the Japanese concept of human nature, the answer is very clear. Human nature is fundamentally good. There is no inherent evil or badness in his basic nature. There are not two worlds, one of *kami* and one of men, one spiritual and the other material. These two worlds interpenetrate and overlap. The visible and the invisible worlds participate in each other. Human beings as the descendants of *kami* have the "flesh" of *kami* in their bodies. There is concrete continuity rather than radical discontinuity. The well-being and happiness of human beings is the same as the well-being and happiness of *kami*. There is no final goal such as a heaven or paradise. The goal is an evolving, dynamic one—the flourishing of all people. Human life is imperfect but human beings are capable of growth. They are not bad. Through rites of purification one can return to his "original shape."

It is basic to Japanese thought to emphasize the essential harmony between man and nature. This does not mean a completely passive attitude toward nature, however. Man should cooperate with nature. Sontoku Ninomiya (1787-1856) recognizes that nature gives of her benefits to some degree only when man works.

"The human way is to repair deserted places and fertilize sterile plains." Nature contantly heals and repairs. "Yet we look to nature, the parent of us all, not as an idle boy looks to his father, but as an industrious boy looks to his father, kind, yet severe in punishment, and eager to recognize the boy's merits. Nature will give no benefit without labour."[8] Even in this relatively modern stress on man being partially over nature, the underlying Shinto sentiment remains.

The basic Japanese life-attitude, reflected in their myth and their history, is one which finds no dualism between spirituality and materiality. All things, including the human appetites, are divine gifts. The enjoyment of them is natural. This explains why even a religion like Buddhism never produced ascetic practices on a wide scale in Japan. There is nothing in Japan to compare to the "five heats" of India when an ascetic sits with a fire burning on each side of himself and a scorching sun overhead. Hajime Naka-mura gives many examples of the Japanese acceptance of the human desires. In ancient Japan love was sensual and extremely free. Drinking, prohibited in early Buddhism, was accepted in Japanese Buddhism. Sexual intercourse while chanting homage to the *Lotus Sutra* was practiced. Near the end of the Heian period, the Tachi-kawa sect of Buddhism identified sexual intercourse with the secret meaning of becoming a Buddha.[9] The disciplines of Bud-dhism were ignored more by the Japanese than by any other group which Buddhism penetrated.

In the Shinto myth there is no estrangement between man and the *kami*. There is no story of a great flood through which deity sought to get rid of evil human beings. There is no Fall and no expulsion from the Garden of Eden. Man is not at war with the *kami* nor is man set against the soil or against woman. Evil is not a cosmic force, though evil or pollution can be contacted in the ordinary course of living. Like dirt or dust, it must be periodically removed, for it can be a handicap to life, blocking life's forward thrust. It is not a corruption of his very being. Specific misdeeds are not the result of willful flouting of divine will, nor is there any punishment inflicted by an offended deity.*

---

* After Chinese influence became strong in Japan, the idea of calamities being a kind of divine punishment spread around. This idea was not a part of Shinto.

The importance of having the right inner attitude also includes having the right attitude toward nature. This is illustrated
by an old tale concerning a rich man who had fields so extensive
no one could see across them. On the day of rice planting, it became
apparent that the task could not be completed before the sun went
down. The rich man thereupon commanded the sun not to set until
the planting was finished. The sun obeyed his bidding and all
seemed to be well. But on the morrow, when people looked out
upon the place where the rich man's fields had been, there was a
great lake extending off into the distance as far as the eye could
reach. Only near the shore could the newly planted rice be seen.

In Shinto one is not expected to coerce or conquer nature;
man seeks to cooperate with it. Similarly one should not attempt
to impose changes upon others or society. The rich man's punishment lay in the fact that nature was no longer essentially friendly
to him since he had sought to compel it to do his will. Each man
should remain in his position, cooperate with nature in all ways
possible with due reverence for the *kami*-element, and cultivate
the right mind-heart, *kokoro*.

The absence of a stern, judgmental approach to life is also
reflected in the absence of anything like a code of law, or Ten
Commandments. This has perplexed many Western scholars.
When the Japanese became aware of this criticism in the last century, some of them devised explanations which were based on
Western assumptions and thus sounded naive. For example, it was
asserted that the ancient Japanese were too good to need any revealed moral laws. However, the explanation is of quite another
kind. The myth which a people accepts about itself and believes in
tells quite a bit about the way the people take hold of experience.
The Semitic mind and the Japanese mind, in their formative
period, simply took hold of experience differently. The difference
must be taken seriously without any premature decision being
made as to which is "better." Certainly the presence of a moral
code alleged to be divinely revealed does not prove a people to
be especially either moral or immoral. Neither does the absence of
such a code.

Lafcadio Hearn's last book on Japan stresses the importance
of ancestor worship in early Japanese society. In such a society, he

holds, there can be no real distinction between religion and ethics, nor between ethics and custom.

> Government and religion are the same; custom and law are identified. The ethics of Shinto were all included in conformity to custom. . . . The true significance of any religious code, written or unwritten, lies in its expression of social duty, its doctrine of the right and wrong of conduct, its embodiment of a people's moral experience. . . . Assuredly the religion of Shinto needed no written commandment: it was taught to everybody from childhood by precept and example, and any person of ordinary intelligence could learn it. When a religion is capable of rendering it dangerous for anybody to act outside of rules, the framing of a code would obviously be superfluous.[10]

However, there are certain basic ideas or concepts that have played a part in the social ethic of Shinto. We shall examine these briefly.

SOCIAL ETHICS OF SHINTO

Most of the basic concepts are related to the mythology and early legends of Japan which deal with the imperial house. The heavenly *kami* ordered Izanagi and Izanami "to make, consolidate, and give birth to this drifting land." This land of heavenly origin is eternal, without end. This conviction became linked with the belief that the emperor's rule would last forever. Centuries ago, a monk named Jichin became intrigued with the idea of the end of the world and wrote that the emperor's rule would end at the one hundredth generation. But Kitabatake Chikafusa (1293-1354), who was living in the reigns of the ninety-sixth and ninety-seventh emperors, held that the one hundred referred to in the phrase *ō-hō-hyaku-dai* meant unlimited. It was this idea which was to prevail in Shinto circles. At the end of World War II, in 1945, many Japanese leaders who struggled to keep the emperor system intact, were influenced by this basic Shinto ideal.

The conviction that the emperor stands in the line of direct descent from Amaterasu by way of the divine grandson, Ninigi-no-mikoto, is also an important element in Shinto. This is linked with the idea of the entire country being like one family under one roof. When the first emperor, Jimmu, chose the spot in the land of Yamato for his capital, he isued an edict in which he said: "We hope to establish a capital from which to unite the whole realm, placing everything under one roof."[11] This expressed the idea of bringing all the diverse tribes under the sway of the men of Yamato. During the recent war with China, the phrase hakkō ichiu* was used to express an idea that would have been inconceivable to people living in the legendary period of Jimmu Tennō. The "roof" was extended to mean the whole world! This using of scriptural texts in wholly unwarranted ways has of course been done elsewhere. For example, one can wonder what the history of the Israelites' conquest of Palestine would have been like told from the point of view of the defeated people, the Canaanites.

Another important Shinto concept is that the relationship between the ruler and the subjects is a fixed one. There can be no reversal in the roles. In Japan's long history, few indeed have been the attempts on the part of a subject to place himself on the imperial throne. The case of the Buddhist priest Dōkyō is famous. The empress Kōken, who reigned from 749 till she abdicated in 758, became very enamored of Dōkyō. There were many disputes around the throne at this time, and even though the empress abdicated she managed to keep much of the power in her own hands—thus she was involved in the disputes. In the fighting that went on in the reign of her immediate successor, Dōkyō's chief enemy was killed. The ex-empress decided to reascend the throne and the emperor was quickly deposed. He was not even given time to change his clothes or put on footgear. Sent into exile with his mother and two or three attendants, he was shortly afterward strangled to death. Dōkyō was thus rid of his most formidable rivals, including the emperor's highest adviser, who at one time had held the affections of the former empress.

Dōkyō was now all-powerful. Although originally he had only been spiritual adviser and physician to the empress, he now

---

* The hakkō of hakkō ichiu means, literally, eight cords or measuring tapes, i.e., everywhere.

Hachiman Jinja. Said to have been founded in 281 A.D. A view of the shrine surrounded by the deep green of the trees. (Kantō region.)

Hachiman Jinja. The shrine protecting the city of Tobata. (Kyūshū region.)

got himself appointed chief minister and gave himself an imperial title, *Hōō*. He lived in the palace along with the empress and plotted how to place himself on the throne. Telling the empress that he had received an oracle from the god Hachiman to the effect that, if he became the ruler of the country, it would enjoy great prosperity, he sought her consent.

At this point the empress had some qualms and she decided to send a loyal courtier to the Hachiman shrine to receive an oracle herself. Wake-no Kiyomaro (732-799), a high-ranking official, was sent. Dōkyō was a shrewd priest-politician and he told Wake-no Kiyomaro that if he brought back a favorable oracle, he could expect to be appointed premier. Otherwise he would be punished severely. Wake-no Kiyomaro was not to be intimidated. The oracle which he received was very clear. "In our country the duties of the Sovereign and the subjects have been determined since the dawn of our history. For a subject to become a ruler is a thing as yet unknown. Without fail set upon the throne one who is of the Imperial Blood. Be ye certain and quick to clear away any malignant person."[12]

The priest Dōkyō was incensed, and severely mutilated Wake-no Kiyomaro before sending him into exile. On his way the emissaries who were on the point of killing Wake-no Kiyomaro, were set upon by wild boars and Wake made his escape. Before Dōkyō could make any successful move the empress had died. It was the influence of Shinto that preserved the throne against a would-be usurper. In the nineteenth century Wake was given the posthumous title of Monarch-Guarding Great-Like Kami and was enshrined at the Go-Ō Shrine in Kyoto.

Throughout the centuries, many of the emperors have been only symbols. But even during the period of military rule through the *shōgun* (which ended in 1867), no one of the military rulers tried to become emperor. The Japanese dynasty is thus probably the oldest continuous dynasty still surviving in the world. The line has remained unbroken. This was facilitated in earlier centuries by the fact that a child of the emperor by any of his consorts was eligible to succeed him. Ponsonby-Fane points out that it is untrue for Western historians to say that the line was kept unbroken only by adoptions. While sons were often adopted, in only one case that Ponsonby-Fane could find did an adopted son come to the throne, named Gohanazono, and even in this case, he was in direct descent from the third Hokuchō sovereign, Suko.[13]

By the Imperial House Law of 1889, only sons of the chief consort can succeed to the throne, and this law lays down a regular order in case there is no direct heir. In the earlier periods primogeniture was not recognized and the choice was made by the reigning sovereign, by one of the high ministers of state, or by one of the retired emperors. Because of this fluidity in procedures, there were frequent backstage maneuvers.

Another important concept is that of the unity of religion and politics, or ritual and government (sai-sei itchi). In ancient times this was probably a fairly common phenomenon in various parts of the world. The same people performed the religious rites who executed the functions of government. In ancient Japan, to serve the kami, to seek for the kami's mind, and to handle political affairs were one and the same. The concept also seems to have included the idea that one should give as serious and honest a heart to political affairs as when one serves the kami at festivals or in rituals.

In the history of the political development of most countries, there comes a time when there is a separation between religion and government, in fact and sometimes also in theory. In Japan the separation in theory did not take place decisively until the Allied Occupation after August, 1945. However, in fact there has been a separation between priestly functions and governmental functions most of the time in her recorded history. When the emperor Sujin (97 B.C.-30 A.D.) removed the sacred mirror and sword from his palace and had them enshrined elsewhere, there was a token separation of religion and government. Even at the present time, the first duties the emperor performs in the early hours of each new year are Shinto rituals, as described in an earlier chapter. The emperor is now only the "symbol" of the state according to the new constitution. But privately he is also the high priest of Amaterasu and he plays an important role in many imperial household rituals pertaining to Shinto. How important

Futara-san Jinja. Mount Futara is worshipped as a sacred mountain; here is enshrined the *kami* credited with the development of the region. (Kantō region.)

Toyosaka-no-mai. A congratulatory dance performed at Shinto wedding ceremonies. Shinto shrines seem to have an increasing popularity as a place for weddings. (Kantō region.)

either of these roles will become in future years it is impossible to predict. Many Japanese feel that the emperor should be termed more than the "symbol" of the state and the discussions concerning constitutional revision will probably continue for a long time.

The above discussion indicates that the Shinto ethic is strongly oriented toward the group. The group is always more important than the individual traditionally. Yet of course there is an individual emphasis also. Great stress is placed on the inner springs of action, motivation, attitude, sincerity. Above all the individual must be sure that he has a pure heart. One reason for visiting the shrine is to be inwardly cleansed. This emphasis on purity of heart or of intention does not mean that one should not think ahead about possible consequences. But the possible consequences never move into the center of the picture. There is no calculating of odds in the mood of the careful gambler. There is no thought of rewards or of punishment, earthly or heavenly. The primary thing is to be sure of the sincerity of one's heart. To be sure, the action itself should be reasonable from beginning to end, so far as one can anticipate such things. But in practice, it is the feeling-tone that receives more attention from the individual than the thinking-through-tone. Many a heroic action is done without any thought of the consequences to oneself, whether in Orient or Occident. The Japanese have traditionally put a high value on heroic action, and if the heart is sincere, many things are forgiven, even actions that prove to be unreasonable in their results. Prince Kaneakira (914-987) taught: "Gods or spirits are just and equable, only accepting a man's religious piety. Go and pray to them with sincerity of heart, and you will be sure to please them.[14] Yamaga-Sokō, known as the founder of the Way of the Warrior (*bushidō*) said: "The first and surest means to enter into communion with the Divine is by sincerity. If you pray to a deity with sincerity, you will surely feel the divine presence."[15]

To live a sincere life and to respect the *kami* comes close to expressing the core of the individual's responsibility. The *kami* at the center of Shinto are ancestral. Ancestor worship was undoubtedly strengthened by the feeling that if the ancestors were kept in a favorable mood, the descendants would prosper. After an agricultural society became basic in ancient Japan, ancestors became a very important factor, since they were thought of as working with the people in the processes of agriculture. Furthermore, once the land was unified under the Yamato rulers who had as their central *kami* Amaterasu, there was a tendency for all the other clans to try to relate their ancestral *kami* to that of the imperial house.

Gradually the idea grew stronger that the emperor's ancestor was the common ancestor of the country. Thus respecting the ancestors came to mean loyalty to the emperor and to the overlords. This concept of loyalty became all-important in the feudal society. During the period of the military knights, or *samurai*, loyalty tended to become the all-inclusive virtue. From the beginning of the Meiji period, 1868, on down to World War II, key officials in government and the armed forces were able to make this loyalty to the emperor the foundation of their crusade for a co-prosperity sphere and a dream of empire. The militarists were able to build upon the strong family feeling of the Japanese with the strong feelings of affection for the emperor, and they used it for their own plans and purposes. No one was encouraged to apply standards of criticism to a system that could be manipulated so easily by the few in control at the top.

What of the place of any sense of guilt in Shinto? Since a Japanese is taught to think of himself only in connection with others, when he feels guilt he is inclined to feel it more as shame than as guilt. But it is a mistake to say that there is no sense of guilt in the Shinto tradition or in the Japanese people. Four key words express the conditions for unity with *kami:* a bright heart, a pure heart, a correct heart, and a straight heart. The opposite of a bright heart is a black heart. Shinto recognizes that people can fall into the state of a black heart. Associated with it is a sense of guilt. However, this sense of guilt is not connected with any concept of supreme goodness. There is no sense of being rejected by *kami* or by nature. There is no sense of *sinfulness*.

Hence it is fairly correct to call Japanese culture a "shame" culture rather than a "guilt" culture, if comparison with the main stream of Christian thinking and feeling is what one has in mind. The links with others in society are all-important to a Japanese. Many of the terms which stand for "man" or "self" or "I" mean "you" when a simple honorific is put in front of them (*jibun, go-jibun; temae, o-temae,* etc.).[16] Man is finite; hence he commits many errors, mistakes, or offenses. The resulting guilt is felt with reference to all one's relationships, both with persons and with *kami.* The purification ceremony is to help one come back into right relations as well as to help one reflect on his behavior.

Here is an ethic that has a distinctly religious dimension but it makes no appeal to any absolute. The method is exploratory and non-dogmatic. There is a recognition of a dimension to the moral life that goes beyond any purely sociological, descriptive category of the reductionistic humanist. The morality of human relationships is rooted in the nature of man as social and as a child of an evolving universe.

CHAPTER EIGHT

The Revival of Shinto and the Meiji Restoration

THE SHINTO RENAISSANCE

At many times in the history of the Japanese people after the formal introduction of Buddhism by the court in the sixth century, the Shinto faith and practice of the masses refused to succumb to the alien influence of Buddhism. Most of the people went on regulating their lives by the rituals of Shinto which centered around the lunar calendar. After approximately one thousand years of *Ryōbu Shinto*, "Dual Aspect Shinto" (an essentially Buddhist way of subordinating the indigenous faith of the people to Buddhist concepts), Shinto was to undergo its most significant renaissance. Among some of the scholars of the eighteenth century a revival of Old Shinto was well underway.

This renaissance of Shinto among the scholars took the form of a return to the Japanese classics and an avoidance of Chinese ideas. At the beginning it consisted largely of a philological study growing out of an interest in the writing of poetry. Philosophically, it sought to reject both Buddhism and Confucianism in the interests of returning to Japan's "ancient purity." Reliance on the *Kojiki* and the *Nihonshoki* came to be paralleled by an emphasis on Amaterasu as the divine foundress of the nation and the ancestress of the imperial house.

One of the great scholars of this movement was Motoori Norinaga (1730-1801). Motoori despised Confucianism, which found its source of authority in the sage. Rather, he held, the source of authority was to be found in the imperial ancestors. All Japanese history was to be viewed as centering upon veneration for the imperial line. Thus Motoori, while fighting against a form of government which he despised, laid the foundation for an almost mystical veneration of the imperial line—later to be used very effectively by the Meiji government to establish another kind of absolutism. One general concept which Motoori developed which was anti-feudal was his thought of the mutual empathy of all natural phenomena (*mono-no-aware*). This phrase cannot be translated literally with any satisfaction. It includes a feeling of intimacy with nature that few Westerners apparently feel ordinarily. It may be illustrated by the words of Fujita Tōko in the nineteenth century:

> The sublime "spirit" of the universe
>   Gathers pure over this Land of the Gods—
> Rising high, it forms the peak of Fuji;
>   Towering aloft, it kisses the skies to a thousand autumns—
> Pouring itself forth out of rivers, it flows as waters of
>   the great deep;
>   And boundless it courses around our Land—
> It blossoms forth as countless clusters of cherry flowers,
>   And naught there is compares to their clustered beauty
>   and scent.
>
> Fujita Tōko (1806–1855)[1]

This stress upon the mutual empathy of all natural phenomena permitted a freer view of human nature than that involved in feudalism.[2] It was also in harmony with the semi-mystical respect for the emperor. Everyman, the islands of Japan, the emperor—all are descended from the *kami*. Confucianism had not been inclined to put any religious fervor into its concept of the "Son of Heaven," the sovereign who ruled by the "Mandate of Heaven" and could be overthrown by the people when he lost the confidence of his subjects. But with the scholars of Old Shinto, the attitude toward the emperor took on religious overtones.

Because of the general conditions prevailing among the masses

of the people in the Tokugawa period (1603-1867), the cult of
Amaterasu as divine ancestress of the emperor and of the nation,
came to play an increasingly important part in the "return to the
past." The Tokugawa government, sometimes described as a
"government by prohibitions," had sought to control every aspect
of the life of the people, even including the styles of dress. It relied
heavily upon a "status ethic" stressed by Confucian scholars.
Each one to his own rank or status! The individual counted for
practically nothing. Filial piety and obedience were the cardinal
virtues. Many ordinary Japanese discovered that their only real
chance for a sense of freedom was to make a pilgrimage to the
shrine of Amaterasu at Ise. All other travel was very strictly controlled. But to get through the "barriers" or governmental check-
points on the highways, all one had to say was that he was making
a pilgrimage to Ise. The common people by the thousands began
to journey to Ise. Although the Tokugawa government had, in
effect, made Buddhism the official religion of the state and required every family to be registered at a Buddhist temple, the
popular movement was in an opposite direction.

By the middle of the nineteenth century, the dissatisfaction
with the Tokugawa government was widespread. Various groups
were actively seeking to end compulsory seclusion of the emperor
in Kyoto and to restore the emperor to active command of the
government. (Since 1185 the emperors had been living in seclusion in Kyoto.) It was being openly said that the Tokugawas
were usurpers of the imperial prerogatives.[3] Leaders of such clans
as the Satsuma, many of whom were personally close to the
emperor in Kyoto, and the Chōshū and others, built upon the
foundations supplied by the scholars of Old Shinto. The divine
origin of the imperial line asserted by these scholars provided a
positive ideal for those interested in a radical change of government. On the negative side, to be capitalized on, was the discon-
tent of the many.

Into this unsettled situation came Commodore Perry in 1853,
inviting Japan to sanction foreign trade. When he returned in
1854 for the reply to the letter from President Fillmore which he
had delivered in the preceding year, the Tokugawa leader (shō-

Tōshō-gū. The Yōmei Gate, depicted here, is one reason why Nikkō is such a famous tourist attraction. It enshrines the soul of the first shōgun of the Edo Bakufu, Tokugawa Ieyasu, and contains the best of the artistic workmanship of the Edo period. (Kantō region.)

gun) was dead. The rule of the Tokugawas went into a rapid decline with some clans ready for outright revolt. By the end of the summer of 1866 the Tokugawa dictatorship was practically over. "The Emperor had selected the advisers for the Shōgun and deprived him of the right to allocate new domains. The powerful clans of Satsuma and Chōshū had openly defied the Shōgun's policies. Civil war had broken out and the rebellious Chōshū forces were openly supporting the Emperor against the Shōgun."[4]

The issue between the rival groups within the party loyal to the imperial cause, whether to return to isolationism or to welcome the opening of the country, was brought to a head by the death of the Emperor Komei on February 3, 1867. He was the last of the anti-foreign emperors. The party favoring broad international relations won out over the conservative, isolationist wing. The new emperor, only a lad, was surrounded by advisers who were to push strongly for modernization. The way was clear for a revolt against the Tokugawas, but the fifteenth and last *shōgun* of the long Tokugawa military government, voluntarily relinquished his title and turned over the reins of government on November 3, 1867, to young Emperor Mutsuhito, later to be known as Emperor Meiji.[5] On December 9, 1867, the command was issued restoring the reins of government to the emperor and the shogunate system was abolished.

SHINTO DURING THE MEIJI PERIOD (1868-1912)

Important as Emperor Meiji was as a person, it was his advisers who played the more crucial roles behind the scenes. These advisers vacillated on the question of whether Shinto was to be treated as a religion or not, but on one thing they remained firm, namely, that Shinto was to be used to give unity and solidarity to the country.[6] This was made all the more necessary because of their desire to modernize Japan as rapidly as possible in order to compete more successfully with the more advanced nations of the world.

On April 5, 1868, a proclamation was issued to the effect

that from then on the government would be based upon a return
to the "Imperial Rule of Jimmu Tennō." On the following day
Emperor Meiji issued the "Imperial Charter Oath of Five
Articles." This can hardly be called the "Magna Charta of the
Japanese Empire," though Nitobe terms it that, since it was
handed down from above; nevertheless, it was a very important
statement of policy.

> An assembly widely convoked shall be established and all meas-
> ures shall be decided by public opinion.
> High and low shall be of one mind, and shall faithfully admin-
> ister the affairs of State.
> All subjects, civil and military officers as well as other people,
> shall have their rights assured and their minds satisfied.
> The uncivilized customs of former times shall be discarded and
> justice and righteousness shall be the basis of all action.
> Knowledge shall be sought for throughout the world and thus
> shall the foundations of our Imperial Polity be strengthened.

To these five points a final paragraph was added. "In order to
perform the greatest reformation in our history, I will lead the
nation in giving an oath to the Kami of Heaven and Earth and will
establish the National Polity to pave the way for Our nation's
security. Ye subjects shall bear this in mind and shall fully cooperate to fulfill this will."[7]

The appeal to the Kami of Heaven and Earth was the first
official indication to the public of the stress to be placed on Shinto
in the new government. It is even more explicit in a letter which
the emperor "wrote" to his people about the same time. "We have
succeeded to the Throne young and weak. Day and night We
wonder how We can maintain Our nation's position among the
other world nations and fulfill the Will of Our Ancestors." Then
follow references to the imperial throne in past periods, the need
to be aware of what is happening in the world, and a final pledge
"together with all Our civil and military officers to abide faithfully by Our Ancestors' great works and will" while bringing
welfare and happiness to "Our one billion subjects and finally
expand over the unlimited span of ocean and waves to bring forth

Hikawa Jinja. Dedicated to the *kami* of the land of Musashi region. The shrine was dedicated as the tutelary shrine of Musashi Province after the capital was transferred from Kyoto to Tokyo at the beginning of the Meiji period. It was here that the Emperor Meiji issued an edict indicating that the unity of religion and government (*saisei itchi*) was to be revived. (Kantō region.)

Aso Jinja. Located at the foot of Mt. Aso. An Inner Shrine (Oku-miya) is located on the mountain top. (Kyūshū region.)

Our national influence, and put Our nation on a foundation solid as a rock." Then follows a plea to the subjects to avoid various doubts and discussions lest the subjects "will not only be depriving Us of Our Way of an Emperor, but would at the same time be losing Our Ancestors' nation. Ye subjects shall firmly bear this in mind, disregard personal opinions and follow public discussions, assist Us in Our work to bring Our nation to security. If Ye subjects shall thus be able to set the Holy Spirits of Our Ancestors at ease, Ye shall do a favor to Us in this world."[8]

Near the end of 1868 the emperor paid a visit to the Hikawa Shrine in Musashi province wherein Tokyo was located, and issued an edict. It read in part: "The worship of the *kami* and regard for ceremonies are the great proprieties of the Empire and the fundamental principles of national polity and education. . . . On this occasion of the restoration, Tokyo has been made the new capital and the Emperor shall reign in person. First of all, rituals shall be initiated and the administration of law and order shall be established. Thus the way of the unity of religion and government (*saisei itchi*) shall be revived."[9]

In a reign which was to become famous because of the rapid spread of many elements of Westernization and modernization, the underlying principle of unity was to be an appeal to the past, to the indigenous religion of Japan, Shinto. At first the effort was to be made to put Shinto into the center as a *religion*. This was to fail for a variety of reasons so that before long it was a "national Shinto" (*Kokka Shinto*) which was put into the center and declared *not* to be a religion. But the underlying policy, that of strengthening reverence for the imperial house, was to remain the same.*

In specific details the Meiji government did a great deal of improvising on the religious question. Having no carefully thought-out plan, it found itself subject to various pressures, from the Buddhists and from foreign governments protesting the discrimination practised against the Christians. But one idea dominated the thinking of its leaders—a government controlled from

---

* The chart of dates at the end of the book will give the reader some idea of the shifts in tactics from 1868 to 1900.

the top and centered in reverence for the emperor. To achieve this end they were willing to engage in a great deal of compromising. Most of the men deciding religious policies were not interested in religion as such, and probably most of them would not even have called themselves religious persons.

Another imperial rescript of 1870, consoling the spirits of the *kami*, follows the same theme as the emperor's previous letter to his subjects.

> We reverently call to mind how that Our Imperial Ancestor, at the time of the founding of the Empire, held the *kami* in high esteem, and loved and cared for the people. The genesis, therefore, of the unity of ceremonial rites and administration is seen in the very distant past. . . . We now repose the spirits of the *kami* of heaven and earth, the spirits of the eight *kami*, and the sacred spirits of the successive Emperors in the Jingi-kan, and so give expression to Our devotion and reverence. We pray that Our subjects throughout the realm may follow this example. It is the nature of the subjects to make this great august Will their own, to receive the spirit of the founding of the Empire as their own by means of ceremonial rites, to pray for the Emperor's peace by sacrificing themselves, and to enhance the spirit of service to the State. . . .[10]

That Shinto was given a central place at the Meiji restoration was natural in view of the influence of Shinto scholars such as Motoori Norinaga and Hirata Atsutane and their followers. These men thought that they had recovered the pure Shinto of the ancient past by their studies of the Japanese classics. They had sought to prove the superiority of the Japanese way to the Chinese way. In China the "mandate of Heaven" had kept changing; there had been many revolutions and thus many dynasties. This reflected a weakness in the Chinese nature, according to these men. In Japan things were quite different. This was because Japan had been founded by the *kami* and governed by the *kami* through their direct descendants, the emperors of a line unbroken from the dim beginnings. Ideas essentially mythic, poetic, and religious in nature were handed over to the politicians for their special purposes. The rebirth of Japanese classical thought thus paved the way for a political use of ideas that were fundamentally religious in nature.

There were very few persons inside Shinto circles who made any strong criticisms of the government's use of Shinto. The chief priest of the Izumo shrine, of the old family of Senge, resisted many of the policies and aroused the violent dislike of the politically-appointed chief priest of the Grand Shrine of Ise. But most of the Shinto priests went along with the government policy and they became government officials in 1872, receiving salaries on condition that they not engage in activities outside the shrines. Those who wanted to engage in religious teaching outside the shrines had to relinquish their government positions.

In the first few years of the Meiji period, when the government was trying to make Shinto the national religion, it was given official status in the government through the Department of Shinto (*Jingi-kan*). Buddhist priests were forced to get out of the shrines, or, if they wished to become Shinto priests, to change their attire immediately. In some sections of the country Buddhists were dealt with very harshly. At Kagoshima, for example, the priest in charge got all the Buddhist monks together at the Kagoshima shrine and had them beaten. In Satsuma, Buddhist temples were burnt. Shrines which made use of Buddhist statues to symbolize Shinto *kami* had to report this to the government. Buddhist implements of worship had to be discarded. Buddhist temple lands were confiscated in February of 1871. Later in that year the government abolished the special ranks which had been given Buddhist temples whose priests had been members of the nobility under the Tokugawas. In some areas the local authorities became over-zealous in their anti-Buddhist measures. The government began to fear extensive riots, so it issued statements saying that the separation of Shinto from Buddhism did not mean that Buddhism was to be destroyed.

The fear of Christianity also plagued some of the government officials. Catholic Christians who had been hidden for over two hundred years on the island of Kyushu made their public appearance near Nagasaki. There were those who feared that Christianity might become a strong religion in Japan. Remembering that the governments of Spain and Portugal had used Christianity as a screen behind which they could interfere in other countries' policies, these people gave expression to their alarm. In 1868 Ono Genshin presented a petition to the court describing the urgent need to prevent the spread of Christianity. Because of this apprehension the government issued an order on May 15, 1868, to all of the clans in the country, saying:

> During the recent revival of Imperial rule, Christianity has begun to spread again and is likely to do great harm to the state. We cannot allow this to continue. Bring the leaders together and explain to them the error of their ways. If they repent, destroy all Christian books and images and have them swear allegiance before the Shinto *kami*. If they refuse to repent, we have no recourse other than to behead a number of the leaders, expose the heads, and to exile the rest to enforced labor in other clans. After a number of years, when they have lost every trace of their faith and when they have manifested complete repentance, they may go home.[11]

Because of pressure from foreign governments, the Japanese government decided not to execute the leaders. All the offenders were sent to distant clans and were put under intensive indoctrination.

In the midst of these difficulties with both Buddhists and Christians, the government went ahead with its efforts to spread Shinto through an Office of Propaganda set up within the Department of Shinto. The government was still having difficulty in formulating a plan, but the disturbances throughout the country and the mounting disappointment of the peasants over their economic plight forced the government into action. In June, 1871, the government took the first step in making Shinto the national religion by issuing the following proclamation.

> The function of shrines is to provide a place of worship for all the people of Japan. They are not the sole property of any individual or family. Some shrines still obtain priests in accordance with ancient procedures, but in most cases the *daimyo* who originally established the shrine has continued to appoint its priests. . . . Priests have become a class apart; this is exactly opposed to unifying worship and

government, and has many harmful effects. . . . From now on, the government will appoint the priests for all shrines, from the very largest at Ise to the very smallest throughout the country.[12]

In January of 1872 the Legislative Bureau suggested that the government was not concentrating enough on spiritual matters. The Bureau suggested that a shrine to Amaterasu be constructed within the palace grounds and that all important affairs of state be decided in front of the shrine. It also recommended the establishment of a Department of Religion and Education, to have the duty of handling all religions, proscribing those religions which opposed established laws. The appointment of teachers, both Shinto and Buddhist, to educate and enlighten the people was recommended. In effect it was being suggested that the government use all the major religions to indoctrinate the people with the official point of view. The "Three Doctrines" of the "Great Teaching" (Dai-kyō) were enunciated:

(1) To embody respect for the kami and love for Japan;
(2) To preach "heavenly reason" and "the way of humanity";
(3) To revere the emperor and to obey his will.[13]

In the following year, June 3, 1873, the government issued explanatory statements for the teaching of the "Three Doctrines," and two lists of topics were prepared for the priests. Many of these topics had nothing to do specifically with religion, such as the duty of paying taxes and the need for rapid modernization. But they reflected the ends of the government in power and the priests were expected to promote the government policy.[14]

The organization which was promoting this "Great Teaching" was called the Dai-kyō-in, "Great Teaching Organization." Leaders from Sectarian Shinto (groups that had personal founders but were not really closely associated with Shinto) as well as from the Buddhist sects were active in this organization. However, the Shinto influence tended to remain dominant. This made for continuing friction. A Buddhist priest of the True Pure Land sect, Shimaji Mokurai, accompanied the Iwakura mission abroad, a mission which went to the United States and to Europe to try to get the 1858 treaties revised. In 1872 this priest sent a letter home requesting the government to cease trying to control religion, and he suggested the abolition of the "Great Teaching Organization." His language clearly reflects the influence of his Western experience.

> In my own opinion, China and Japan have frequently confused government and religion. Europeans have also erred on this point. As a result, they have harmed their culture greatly. There have been many improvements in the Western world, however. I had hoped that the same improvements would take place in Japan, but apparently just the opposite is happening. Let me mention briefly one or two points on which I disagree. The first of the Three Doctrines enjoins reverence towards the gods and patriotism. Reverence towards the gods is religion, patriotism is government. Is this not confusing religion and government?[15]

Other priests who had been abroad were to support the position stated by Shimaji Mokurai. Certain changes were brought about in 1873. Shinto priests were removed from local or national government payrolls if they wanted to teach religion. The compulsory registration at Shinto shrines was abolished (an idea borrowed from the Tokugawa government, which had required every family to be enrolled at a Buddhist temple as a part of its system of control). Late in 1873 the government admitted that its attempt to make Shinto the national religion had failed. "The government shall protect the freedom of both Shinto and Buddhism and shall encourage each of them to grow. This will make them an administrative asset rather than liability to the nation. This is the attitude of the government toward priests; it gives the priests religious freedom."[16]

In May, 1875, the government abolished the *Dai-kyō-in* and gave up the effort to promote a new religion. Theoretically the religions were now all equal. However, the government lifted one strand from traditional Shinto thought, the reverence for the emperor and his divine ancestors, and this was to be made into a "cult of patriotism" which was to succeed all too well—up to the great defeat of 1945.

The official position that Shrine Shinto was not to be regarded as a religion at all was made clear in April, 1900, when two separate offices were created, one the Office of Shrines and the other the Office of Religions. This gave Shinto a special status which pleased most of the Shinto priests. Shrine worship was declared to be not a religion, but rather reverence for the emperor and the imperial ancestors. Thus it was obligatory on all Japanese. This office and definition were to last until the end of World War II in 1945.

THE MEIJI CONSTITUTION AND THE IMPERIAL RESCRIPT ON EDUCATION

Two other documents or events in the Meiji period having great significance for Shinto must be referred to. On February 11, 1889, the emperor gave to his subjects a constitution. The imperial rescript which accompanied it included the statement, "With the August Powers bequeathed by Our Ancestors, We promulgate this everlasting great Constitution to Our subjects as of today and tomorrow. Our Ancestors have established this Empire with the cooperation and assistance of the ancestors of Our subjects, and bequeathed it eternally to Us."

Before the spirits of his ancestors and the *kami*, the emperor also took an oath before the sanctuary in the imperial palace.

> We, the Successor to the prosperous Throne of Our Predecessors, do humbly and solemnly swear to the Imperial Founder of Our House and to Our other Imperial Ancestors that, in pursuance of a great policy coextensive with the Heavens and the Earth, We shall maintain and secure from decline the ancient forms of government.[17]

Articles One and Three of the Meiji Constitution reveal the influence of the Shinto myth. "The Empire of Japan shall be reigned over and governed by a line of Emperors unbroken for ages eternal." "The Emperor is sacred and inviolable." Prince Itō, who played an important part in the drafting of the constitution, wrote in his *Commentaries on the Constitution*:

> The Sacred Throne was established at the time when the heavens and the earth became separated. The Emperor is Heaven descended, divine and sacred; He is preeminent above all his subjects. He must be reverenced and is inviolable. He has indeed to pay due respect to the law, but the law has no power to hold him accountable to it. Not only shall there be no irreverence for the Emperor's person, but also He shall not be made a topic of derogatory comment nor one of discussion."[18]

The Imperial Rescript on Education, issued on October 30, 1890, was also to play a tremendous part in the cult of emperor reverencing. The rescript grew out of the growing awareness on the part of the government that Westernization was proceeding at such a pace that many Japanese were despising anything that was considered traditional. The author of the rescript was the Minister of Education, Yoshikawa Akimasa, but he consulted the emperor frequently in the course of its composition. Most of the content of the rescript is taken up with the four virtues of benevolence, righteousness, loyalty, and filial piety, which the author admitted were drawn from the Chinese tradition. "But I strongly upheld the teaching of these four principal virtues, saying that the essence of man's morality is one and the same irrespective of place or time, although it might take different forms according to different circumstances, and that therefore the aforesaid four virtues could well be made the moral standard of the Japanese people."[19]

The official translation of the rescript follows.

Know Ye, Our Subjects:

> Our Imperial Ancestors have founded Our Empire on a basis broad and everlasting and have deeply and firmly implanted virtue; Our subjects ever united in loyalty and filial piety have from generation to generation illustrated the beauty thereof. This is the glory of the fundamental character of Our Empire and herein also lies the

source of Our Education. Ye, Our Subjects, be filial to your parents, affectionate to your brothers and sisters; as husbands and wives be harmonious; as friends be true; bear yourselves in modesty and moderation; extend your benevolence to all; pursue learning and cultivate arts, and thereby develop intellectual faculties and perfect moral powers; furthermore, advance public good and promote common interests; always respect the Constitution and observe the laws; should emergency arise, offer yourselves courageously to the State; and thus guard and maintain the prosperity of Our Imperial Throne coeval with heaven and earth. So shall ye not only be Our good and faithful subjects, but render illustrious the best traditions of your forefathers.

The Way here set forth is indeed the teaching bequeathed by Our Imperial Ancestors to be observed alike by the Descendants and the subjects, infallible for all ages and true in all places. It is Our wish to lay it to heart in all reverence in common with you, Our Subjects, that we may all attain to the same virtue.[20]

The Rescript on Education was to provide the unifying ideology for the educational system of the nation in behalf of "national Shinto." The government already had approximately 200,000 shrines under its control. Now the students were to be properly indoctrinated with respect for the emperor and "the kami way."[21] The document was treated with a respect approaching religious awe. All schools had copies of the rescript and there was a yearly ceremony at which it was read while everyone bowed reverentially.

The opening phrase of the rescript, "Our Imperial Ancestors," was written so as to indicate two classes of ancestors—those preceding the first human emperor as well as those following him. The Department of Education commentary on these words makes this very clear: "The kami-gami, beginning with Amaterasu Omikami, who laid the foundations of the imperial glory, and Jimmu Tennō, who established his authority over the country, spread abroad the imperial influence and was the first human emperor."[22] Hence the Shinto myth was deliberately tied in with both the legendary and the historical periods as having the same substance or value.

The emphasis on the importance of lineage was not something invented by the Meiji government. It has always been a strong element in Japanese society since its earliest recorded events. The element of awe surrounding the emperor was also of ancient tradition. A monk named Kenko had written many years before the Meiji period: "The Imperial Throne of the Mikado inspires us with the greatest awe; even the uttermost leaf of the Imperial Family Tree is worthy of honour and very different from the rest of mankind. The world is declining to its end . . . but there is cause for satisfaction in the fact that the venerable palace is still uncontaminated by the outer world."[23] In the fourteenth century Kitabatake Chikafusa had written: "Our Imperial Ancestor for the first time set the foundation of the nation, and Amaterasu forever handeth on the Imperial Throne. This is a thing existing only in our country and without parallel in foreign lands. This is why we call it a Land of the Gods."[24] And Motoori Norinaga wrote: "The doctrine relating to Amaterasu Omikami looks simple on the surface, but as a matter of fact, it is to be recognized as exceedingly profound."[25]

This use of myth for political purposes was surrounded with the garb of constitutionalism and the external features of Westernization. The emotions to which it appealed, to help in the creation of a sense of national solidarity, were ancient ones, tied in with one aspect of Shinto. The Tokugawa government had tried to maintain a rigid society based on social class, rank, strict Confucian principles, and non-fraternization with outside forces. The Meiji government, by contrast, stressed contact with the outside world yet at the same time emphasized the centrality of the emperor and the *mystique* of the divine ancestry. The appeal to myth was an appeal to deep feelings in the Japanese. Rationally out of line with the Westernized slant of the Meiji advisers, realistically it proved a very good device for keeping the people in their place as *subjects*. What nationalism does not live, for many of its most ardent followers, in and through a myth that has no rational connection with the earthiness of politics?

Every society and every group of rulers has to find some way of mediating between the past and the future. In a period of extremely rapid transition, such as Japan went through after 1868, a balance wheel was needed to keep things from flying in all directions. The cult of ancestor worship became that balance wheel for the Meiji government. Prior to Meiji, ancestor worship had centered in the domestic cult and in the worship of the tutelary *kami* of clans or places. Under the Tokugawas, ancestor worship had been wedded to the patterns of feudalism and the Confucian ethic, and thus lent itself readily to a hierarchical type of society. The spirit of the past controlled the present in many ways in the period of the Tokugawas.

In a similar way the spirit of the past was to control the masses in the Meiji period and after, but this time in behalf of achieving a place in the community of great nations and by means of modern military techniques. When appeal to the past is used as a tool of authoritarian control from the top, it makes for rigidity and an inability to criticize present policies and present social structures intelligently and openly. Shinto, which in itself is not rigid, was made into something quite rigid by her political manipulators. The Meiji government, and later the military clique which gained increasing power, wanted to keep most of the people "in their places." Only a small group at the top should have real power. The others must obey.

In effect, the Meiji government incorporated much of the older feudalism into its own policies as far as its control of the masses was concerned. The loyalty which had formerly been directed toward feudal clan chiefs was now to be directed solely to the emperor whom they themselves controlled. Shinto religious sentiments were used for non-religious ends, a pattern which many other governments have, of course, followed with reference to other religious traditions.

It is part of the tragedy of Shinto in the Meiji period that it was not able to come to vocal self-consciousness. If there had been Shinto thinkers in high positions who could have spoken out against the distorting of the tradition, the history of Japan in the next hundred years would have been considerably different, without a doubt. But it was not the genius of Shinto to be either self-conscious or vocal.

Within a space of fifty years, the men around Emperor Meiji and his successor were able to transform a society which had lived in isolation for over two centuries into an influential world power. They developed an industrial and military potential that was able to defeat both China and Russia, events which forced the West to take a new look at this island nation. These same Japanese leaders appealed to the feudal sentiments of loyalty but they were able to use it in behalf of their plans for modernization. The outward transformation of Japan gave her a superficial resemblance to the nations of the West with their emphasis upon the importance of the individual person. But inwardly the Japanese went on living by the myths and symbols of the past, tied to the group-mind and manipulated rather shrewdly by the men at the top. The feudal attitudes were not dead. Neither was Shinto dead. But the Shinto that emerged as a cult of patriotism was a far cry from the Shinto of the peasant, of the village, of the agricultural festivals with their feeling for the mystery of growth.

CHAPTER NINE

Background to Disaster: 1912-1945

What began in the Meiji period was to continue down through the Taishō period, which ended in 1926, and into the first twenty years of the Shōwa era. Millions of Japanese were conditioned to think that Shinto was what the militarists and nationalists had made of it—a cult of patriotism and loyalty centering in the concept of the divine origin of the imperial line. The "Imperial Way" (*kōdō*) was interpreted as identical with the "Way of the Kami" (*kannagara-no michi*). The people were taught that the emperor and Amaterasu were identical, "of one august body."[1]

The version of the national history used in the 1930's in ordinary primary schools, prescribed by the Department of Education, was quite simple. Amaterasu had sent down from heaven her grandson, Ninigi-no-mikoto, to subdue the rough forces in the Japanese islands and to rule them. He was given the Three Sacred Treasures, the mirror, the sword, and the jewels. These signs of imperial power were passed on at the end of the Divine Ages (variously said to have lasted for from three thousand years to over a million years) to the first human emperor, Jimmu Tennō. According to the *Nihonshoki*, Jimmu Tennō said: "I think that this land will undoubtedly be suitable for the extension of the Heavenly task, so that its glory should fill the universe. It is, doubtless, the center of the world."[2]

The superiority of the Japanese nation and her people, emphasized in these primary school textbooks of that period, is traced to this unbroken lineage with its divine ancestry. The kind of interpretation popular in the 1930's is reflected in the Japanese writer Yasubumi Fukusaku. Listing three elements that enter into the establishment of successful control over a people—power, moral excellence, and lineage—he puts the stress on lineage. For power can be defeated by other power, and moral excellence is hard to evaluate properly. But no human power can affect lineage. Lineage imparts an

> absolute quality to the status of ruler. The ruler is ruler forever and the subjects are subjects forever, and the great moral obligation existing between the ruler and his people is never in any way confused. . . . Not only is the Throne made secure and unchanging, but also the national life is made secure and unchanging. We cannot avoid being deeply impressed by the divine intelligence and moral excellence revealed by our national ancestress, Amaterasu Omikami, in the attention which she paid to this point. She did not rely on moral excellence, nor on power, but on lineage. . . . Our national head, whom we name with deepest reverence, was a woman who was possessed of a remarkably penetrating intelligence. . . .[3]

The schools, teachers, and textbooks emphasized the "historical" interpretation of the ancient myth. Textbooks showed genealogical tables tracing the origin of the imperial house all the way back to Izanagi and Izanami. People who knew better learned to remain silent because of the "thought control" police. The great majority went along with the governmental position that "the land of Japan stands high above the other nations of the world, and her people excel the peoples of the world." They went along because they were given no chance to know anything different.

The resort to mythical language to support the national cause was one more way in which the Japanese were imitating the nations of the West. Had not the American nation only a few decades earlier talked in terms of "manifest destiny" when it engaged in a war with Spain? Were there not in existence in the West textbooks which claimed that the Caucasian race was the only race that had a history worth recording? The leaders of Nazi Germany and Fascist Italy had appealed to their racial myths to justify crimes against their fellowmen. Twentieth-century man was to discover again that men will live and die for myths when they have been sufficiently indoctrinated. The Japanese leaders were doing essentially what many other national leaders were doing or had done. Many of the large-scale crimes committed against humanity are done in the name of myth or religion. The disease is by no means cured yet.

By the opening of the 1930's, for most Japanese Shinto had become completely identified with the national cause. From September 18, 1931, until August 15, 1945, Japan was to be in a state of war. In September 1931 Japanese troops invaded Manchuria, ousting the military governor, Chang Hsueh-liang. The army had seized the initiative. By October of that year rumors were spreading through official circles in Tokyo that the people responsible for the Manchurian affair were planning to come back to Tokyo to carry out a *coup d'état*.[5] This was the beginning of a long period of tension in which the army gradually came to play the dominating role in the formulation and execution of policy. The army moved increasingly into the center but, at the same time, it tried to avoid the appearance of a military dictatorship.[6]

There were people with mental reservations but there was no group protest. Religious organizations, old and new, went along with the state. Shinto had been made into a handmaiden of the state. Some shrines became increasingly important, such as the Yasukuni Shrine, which honored the souls of those who died in battle. A general was appointed its head priest. The Hachiman shrines became more important because of their association with a *kami* of war. The officially promoted *mystique* regarding the emperor and his divine ancestors made it practically impossible for any rational criticism from within the ranks of Shinto leaders. The Buddhists also participated in the national drive, making collections for the purchase of airplanes. "Ultranationalistic movies were promoted by Buddhist organizations. Nichiren priests attained a special reputation for chauvinism. Certain temples appear to have been rendezvous for some of the most ultranationalistic schemers."[7] Of far greater significance were patriotic societies which were devoted to achieving a combination of the "imperial way" and Buddhist doctrines. The Japanese began to believe that they could prevail over all odds. The "spirit" of the nation would defeat the factories and armed might of their enemies. Religious groups furthered this kind of thinking.

THE "NATIONAL POLITY" (KOKUTAI)

On March 30, 1937, the Ministry of Education published an official statement of the Japanese theory of the state called the *Kokutai-no Hongi*. It was issued in tremendous quantities. In the first two years almost two million official copies were sold and there were thousands of private reprints. It was to be used as a guidebook for teachers of courses in ethics.[8] This document based itself largely on an appeal to Shinto ideals and ideas as interpreted since the time of Meiji. Frequently it referred to Emperor Meiji's Rescript on Education, issued forty-seven years before.

The book was written in a style that made it difficult reading for the average person. However, its acceptance was ensured by its being issued by the Bureau of Thought Control in the Ministry of Education. This Bureau, by working closely with the police, had been responsible in one decade for the arrest of more than 60,000 people for "unacceptable thoughts." The book was an argument against the "false doctrines of individualism." "Individualism" was a term which covered almost anything that the Bureau of Thought Control felt might be a threat to the national cause as defined by the militarists. Socialism, anarchism, and communism were all grouped under the term "individualism," as well as what might more normally (by Western standards) be called individualism. To be an individualist in the 1930's meant to be a threat to the state, and this bordered on treason.

Did most of the Japanese "believe" in the ideas in this document? This is a Western-type question. To a Japanese, belief is much less important than feeling. The language of the *Kokutai-no Hongi* is often effusive and emotional. Its appeal to "a Japanese way of life" different from all others and superior to them, is an appeal to feelings, not to rationality. Every nation at one time or another becomes bewitched by such feelings. When Japanese talk and write about their cultural superiority, it is hard to know which element is stronger, feelings of superiority or feelings of inferiority. The acceptance of the basic philosophy underlying the *Kokutai-no Hongi* was more in the nature of an uncriticized religious faith than of any rational acceptance at the level of belief.

The author of the *Kokutai-no Hongi* states his purpose very clearly in his introduction. "This book has been compiled in view of the pressing need of the hour to clarify our national entity [or polity] and to cultivate and awaken national sentiment and consciousness. . . . We must return to the standpoint peculiar to our country, clarify our immortal entity . . . bring into being the original condition. . . ."⁹ The eternal and immutable national polity is then stated as being "the unbroken line of Emperors, receiving the Oracle of the Founder of the nation, reigning eternally over the Japanese Empire." Enkindled by this principle, "all the people, united as one great family nation in heart and obeying the Imperial will, enhance indeed the beautiful virtues of loyalty and filial piety."¹⁰

The government is a sacred undertaking in that the emperor "on the one hand worships the spirits of the Imperial Ancestors and on the other as deity incarnate (*akitsu-mi-kami*) leads his people." When the emperor is called "deity incarnate—marvellous deity—or humanly manifested deity," this is not to be taken as having any reference to "the so-called absolute God or omniscient and omnipotent God." It signifies "that the Imperial Ancestors have manifested themselves in the person of the Emperor, who is their divine offspring, that the Emperor in turn is one in essence with the Imperial Ancestors. . . ."¹¹ It is through his religious functions that the emperor becomes one in essence with the imperial ancestors. At the same time he functions as father to his children, whom he loves and protects "as one would sucklings and, depending upon their cooperation, diffuses his policies widely." The subjects should cast themselves aside and serve the emperor intently.¹²

Casting oneself aside means entering into a kind of non-personal state. The author describes it as that "between non-personalities," involving self-effacement and "a return to the 'one,' " that is, to the one great way. By sweeping aside the corruption of the spirit and the clouding of knowledge that follows upon thinking upon one's self, one should return "to a pure and clear state of mind that belongs intrinsically to us as subjects, and thereby fathom the great principle of loyalty. This patriotism is united at the roots with loyalty and with reverence for the *kami* and the ancestors."[13]

Harmony is also stressed. Through their toil and labor individuals harmonize into one. Where there is harmony, there is growth, creation. The way of harmony should be expressed in all aspects of life. This means cultivating a heart which does not follow its own wishes. Each subject is to seek a pure and cloudless heart, a heart which dies to one's ego and one's own need. "That means, it is a heart that lives in the way of unity between the Sovereign and his subjects, a Way that has come down to us ever since the founding of the Empire. . . . The spirit that sacrifices self and seeks life at the very fountainhead of things manifests itself eventually as patriotism and as a heart that casts aside self in order to serve the State."[14]

When the author of the *Kokutai-no Hongi* is dealing with the emperor Meiji's bestowing of the constitution, he idealizes this process, saying nothing about the various forces that were at work in the decade preceding its appearance. Only in other countries, according to the author, have constitutions emerged as the result of contending forces or a struggle for power. The Japanese constitution was granted by the throne and "instituted in perfect accord with his great august Will by virtue of the 'supreme authority bestowed upon him by the Imperial Ancestors.' " In his terms, the constitution was "nothing short of an Imperial Edict."[15]

As to where the supreme power lies, the *Kokutai-no Hongi* is very clear. It is in the emperor. "The theory which holds the view that sovereignty lies in essence in the State and that the Emperor is its organ has no foundation except for the fact that it is a result of blindly following the theories of Western states." The emperor is not a sovereign like those in foreign countries but reigns over Japan as "a deity incarnate." The Japanese Diet is not a representative organ of the people, as in other countries, but simply a means of assisting the emperor's direct rule in special ways. "Hence, all our laws find their source in the Emperor's august virtue."[16]

This was the document issued by the Bureau of Thought Control in the Ministry of Education in 1937. All power was traced

to the emperor at a time when actually he had become virtually a
victim or prisoner of the military clique. That the Japanese army
initiated many of its major moves, from the opening incident in
Manchuria in September, 1931, to the surprise attack on Pearl
Harbor in December, 1941, without even consulting the emperor,
is now pretty well established.[17] The myth of the divine origin of
the throne was a convenient screen behind which the militarists
could hide while molding the people into a conformist state of
mind. Centuries of feudalism and the rigid, hierarchical ideas of
Confucianism had not made it possible for individuals to emerge
who could rigorously criticize the system of which they were a
part. There were not lacking intellectuals like the former professor
in the law department at Tokyo University who could write in
1919: "Subjects have no mind apart from the will of the Emperor."[18]

The responsibility of Shinto and Shinto leaders for Japan's
recourse to a totalitarian society was overstressed in books written
in the 1940's by non-Japanese. This is not to deny the obvious
fact that, in history, religions have often lent themselves to the
leaders who launch crusades by using religious slogans. The appeal
is always non-rational, whether to the "will of God" or the will of
the sovereign. The quasi-religions of modern times like Marxism
and Fascism are just as subject to irrational appeals and irrational
faith. But it should be remembered that Japanese religious leaders
of all faiths tended to behave in essentially the same way after
Japan was in a state of war. As far as the long history of Shinto is
concerned, a case can be readily made that it has been a more
peaceful religion than either Christianity or Islam. But the crucial
question for modern men everywhere is not about the past history
of the religions (or their modern militant substitutes), all of which
are as earth-born as anything else mankind's societies produce;
but whether any of the religions, old or new, will provide intelli-
gent, dynamic leadership in a world that is still suffering from
hyper-nationalism. Or are the religions of mankind destined to
become only interesting museum pieces?

CHAPTER TEN

Shrine Shinto Since 1945

Disaster struck in August, 1945. The nation which had never suffered defeat in a war went down to an almost total collapse. Many Japanese were hoping for the ending of the war, but up to the very end, there were faithful Japanese who were ready to use the sword of the spirit against the armed might of her enemies. The dedication of many of these Japanese was something which many Westerners have found hard to understand. Over four years ago I became fairly well acquainted with an older Shinto priest in the Osaka area. He shared with me some of his experiences from the war period as we talked about Shinto and its prospects. He told me of his first interview with the American Occupation officer in his area. He was one of the few priests who spoke English, and probably for that reason was sent for as speedily as possible after the Occupation had settled down for business in the Osaka area.

The American army officer was interested in what the priests and his associates had been doing in the last weeks of the war. The Shinto priest told him that he and his friends had gone down to the harbor night after night, standing watch throughout the night with bamboo spears.

"But didn't you know we had landing boats, machine guns, aircraft?" asked the American officer. "We could have shot you down before you could use a single bamboo spear."

"What difference does that make?" the Shinto priest replied. "We were there to defend the emperor and our country. We knew we would die."

It is the heart that counts, he was saying, the true and pure heart that knows only loyalty to the end. The results do not matter. The priest had given his wife a dagger with which she promised to kill herself as soon as the invaders had forced their way ashore. She, too, intended to die out of loyalty to the emperor. It was this kind of dedication without any calculating of the results that often puzzled Westerners.

But the expected invasion of Japan did not come. My friend with his bamboo spear was not shot down and his wife, who worked with him as priestess in the Shinto shrine, did not have to commit suicide. To all of his subjects the emperor of Japan spoke by radio, asking them to accept the inevitable. Aside from a few episodes, the entire nation submitted, simply because the emperor had spoken.

Four months after the ending of the war, on December 15, 1945, the Supreme Commander for the Allied Powers in Tokyo forwarded to the Imperial Japanese Government a document with the title "Abolition of Governmental Sponsorship, Support, Perpetuation, Control, and Dissemination of State Shinto." This is referred to more briefly as the "Shinto Directive." This grew out of conferences with interested Japanese officials, but back of it lay the general statement of policy on Shinto as laid down by the Department of State of the United States Government.[1]

The problem which the Occupation authorities faced was not a simple one. Probably in no other modern state is the head of state as deeply involved as the Japanese emperor in religious rites and ceremonies which express not only the personal faith of the sovereign himself but also the basic feelings, if not the faith, of the nation as a nation. The Japanese people had not enjoyed genuine religious freedom under the Meiji constitution. Now they were to be offered religious freedom as understood in the Western countries. As one writer has pointed out, "If the Emperor was to be permitted to continue as the temporal leader of the Japanese, how could he be stripped of his ecclesiastical position without an infringement upon his personal religious rights and those of his loyal followers? How could the masses of the Japanese people be delivered from the ideological bondage and financial burden of State Shinto without violating the personal religious liberties of the millions who apparently held this philosophy as a religious faith? How could an attack be made on a pernicious ideology without religious persecution?"[2]

That the Shinto Directive could not handle all of these issues goes without saying. The announced purpose of the Directive was "to separate religion from the state, to prevent misuse of religion for political ends, and to put all religions, faiths, and creeds upon exactly the same basis, entitled to precisely the same opportunities and protection." In addition, it made a direct attack upon the essence of the official philosophy of the nation as summed up in the *Kokutai-no Hongi*. The circulation of this book by the government was specifically prohibited.*

Many of the issues raised by the Shinto Directive are still to be faced. However, it is now up to the Japanese people themselves to make whatever changes they feel are called for. The American voice is no longer a part of the discussions in Japanese circles. That some of the issues are not being discussed more openly now is traceable to the fact that Shinto leaders do not want to say anything which might bring the Communists out in even stronger attacks upon the emperor system. At present there is a tendency to "wait and see."

As a result of the Directive, "State Shinto" was abolished and Shrine Shinto was recognized as a religion, entitled to the same protection as any other religion. Formerly Shinto shrines had received support from the government, national or local. From now on all support for the shrines was to be private and voluntary. The Grand Shrine of Ise, main shrine of Amaterasu, ancestress of the imperial house, became a private shrine. No public educational institution could teach Shinto doctrine or train men for the Shinto priesthood. This meant the abolishment of the Shinto university at Ise Shrine, which was founded in 1882 and became a professional school in 1902 under the jurisdiction of the Home Ministry. In

---

* Much of what happened in the conferences between Occupation officials and Japanese persons concerning religious policies formulated at that time, is yet to be written. Mr. William Woodard, of the International Institute for the Study of Religions, Tokyo, was in a key spot in the Occupation office dealing with religious affairs. A book he is writing, dealing with religion under the Allied Occupation, based upon all available official documents and interviews with the key Japanese persons still living, is forthcoming. Mr. Woodard kindly allowed me to look at portions of his material in preparation.

1940 it had been raised to the status of university and put under the jurisdiction of the Education Ministry. The Shrine Board in the Ministry of Home Affairs was abolished.[3] The favored position which Shinto had received as a "non-religion" from the end of the Meiji era till 1945 was ended. The Buddhists, who had enjoyed a favored position prior to the rise of the Meiji government, could at least rejoice in this change. Many Shinto priests, however, found themselves in a confused situation emotionally and in bad straits economically.

At the end of 1945 an ordinance that enabled religious institutions to become juridical persons was issued. One by-product of this was the proliferation of many branch organizations from Shinto, Buddhism, and Christianity, as well as the emergence of many new religious organizations "like bamboo shoots after the rain."[4]

EMPEROR'S RESCRIPT, JANUARY 1, 1946

Another very important step pertaining to Shinto was taken by the emperor on January 1, 1946, in his New Year's Rescript. Just what went on behind the scenes here has not yet been written in detail. It is not the custom for imperial rescripts to be written by the emperors. Hence, from the documents themselves it is not possible to say how much the mind of any given emperor is reflected. Many Japanese still seem to think that the rescript which "demythologized" the emperor was the result of pressure from Occupation officials. Others believe it was a result of efforts on the part of some of the Japanese officials to "get in ahead" of the Occupation on this issue, and was not unrelated to the desire of these Japanese to do nothing which would jeopardize the position of the emperor or the emperor system.

By the opening of 1946, what was to be done about the emperor and the emperor system had not been revealed by the Occupation authorities. If the Japanese hoped to head off very strict or drastic measures which they thought the Occupation officials might introduce, their action was certainly understandable and reasonable. The Americans, for their part, wanted to avoid producing the wrong results by ill-advised actions. Until certain documents are uncovered or diaries of conversations are published, it is quite possible to believe that the basic ideas in the rescript expressed the convictions of the emperor himself, even though some suggestion regarding a public pronouncement may have come from someone high up in the Occupation. In any event, the rescript was received with satisfaction by the Allies.

The rescript opens with a restatement of five points of the Charter Oath of Emperor Meiji.

> We wish to take this oath anew and restore the country to stand on its own feet again. . . . Keeping in close touch with the desires of the people, we will construct a new Japan through thoroughly being pacific, the officials and the people alike obtaining rich culture and advancing the standard of living of the people. . . . Love of the family and love of country are especially strong in this country. With more of this devotion should we now work toward love of mankind. . . .

> We stand by the people and we wish always to share with them in their moments of joys and sorrows. The ties between us and our people have always stood upon mutual trust and affection. They do not depend upon mere legends and myths. They are not predicated on the false assumption that the Emperor is divine and that the Japanese people are superior to other races and fated to rule the world. . . .[5]

Three items stand out in this document. One is the emperor's denial of the conception that the emperor is divine, coupled with the statement that the ties binding the emperor and the people do not depend upon mere legends and myths. Another is the denial of the conception that the Japanese people are superior to other races and fated to rule the world. The third important item is the emperor's statement that the Japanese should work toward love of mankind, not just toward love of family and country.

This rescript has been described by Hall as "the final step in officially discarding the basic ideology which is expressed in the *Kokutai-no Hongi*"; and he sees the emperor as electing "to retain his position as political leader of his people and to discard his dual role as religious leader."[6] I fail to see that the emperor discarded his role as religious leader except as that had been defined by a certain type of ultra-nationalism. In this rescript Emperor Hirohito ruled out certain "false conceptions" of his own role, but he did not and could not rule out the significant part he plays in the living stream of Shinto, symbolized by his frequent participation in Shinto rites or *matsuri*. Legally, he does not participate in these rites in his official capacity but only as a private individual. However, in the light of my own contact with many Shinto priests outside of the big cities, I doubt very much if the average Japanese peasant or villager is too aware of this distinction. What is done with this "legal fiction" by the Japanese leaders themselves remains to be seen. So long as the vocal Communists threaten to do away with the emperor system, there will be little public discussion of the emperor and his religious role.

A NEW CONSTITUTION

On November 3, 1946, a new constitution was promulgated which went into effect on May 3, 1947.[7] Article 20 of this new constitution states:

Freedom of religion is guaranteed to all. No religious organization shall receive any privileges from the state, nor exercise any political authority. No person shall be compelled to take part in any religious act, celebration, rite or practice. The State and its organs shall refrain from religious education or any other religious activity.

The Meiji constitution of 1889 had presumed to give religious freedom, but it was made conditional on the subject's being loyal to his emperor, who was declared to be "sacred and inviolable." This mixing of political and religious categories is absent from the new constitution. Religious organizations are free to carry on religious activities without interference from the government. Individuals may practice freedom of choice in their religious affiliations. Shinto has been separated from the state and has its own organization, the Association of Shinto Shrines (*Jinja Honchō*). The state no longer requires financial support for Shinto. Contributions are voluntary. Shinto observances are no longer a part of the public educational system.[8]

The position of the emperor is also changed in the new constitution. According to the opening articles:

1. The Emperor shall be the symbol of the State and of the unity of the people, deriving his position from the will of the people with whom resides sovereign power.
2. The Imperial Throne shall be dynastic and succeeded to in accordance with the Imperial House Law passed by the Diet.

Here it is explicitly stated that sovereignty lies with the people, a view regarded as heretical in the Meiji period and in the *Kokutai-no Hongi*. Does this mean that the national polity (*kokutai*) has been changed? The debate on this continues. In November, 1946, a statement was published by the Japanese Cabinet called "Exposition on the New Constitution." It gives the government's explanation concerning the national polity and sovereignty. Following are the crucial passages from that booklet. The Cabinet's purpose was "to introduce the Government's explanation and to leave the matter to individual judgment."

According to the Cabinet's statement, national entity (the Cabinet's word for *kokutai*, or polity) is defined as meaning basic characteristic of the nation. So defined, the national entity has not been changed. But to those for whom the forms of government constitute the national entity, it has undergone a great change through the late revision. By defining the national entity as the basic characteristic of the nation, the Cabinet statement adds: "So interpreted, national entity forms the foundation of the nation's existence, and its destiny is common with that of the State; so that if this national entity were to suffer change or loss, the State would

at once lose its existence." Under such circumstances "we would
have to conclude that even if a new State were to be established,
there would no longer be anything common in the nature of the
old State and the new." Looking upon national entity in this way
and in relation to Japan specifically, the Cabinet states that national entity "in a word means the immutable and solemn fact
that the Japanese people look up to the Emperor as if he were the
center of their adoration, on the basis of the link that deep down
in their hearts binds them to him, that the entire nation is united
thereby, and that this forms the basis of Japan's existence."[9] In
other words, there has been no change in the national entity.

The Cabinet statement then turns to the other view held by
many scholars in theory of law, according to which Articles I to IV
of the Meiji constitution are "a so-called stipulation of our national
entity." This attitude the Cabinet statement regards as showing
a certain bondage to institutional characteristics that have varied
with the times since the days of Meiji. These things should be
understood as belonging properly only to *forms of government*,
not to the national entity. However, if national entity is identified
with forms of government, then of course the national entity has
undergone a great change through the recent revision of the constitution.

In contrast to the position taken by some of the people in the
field of the theory of law, the Cabinet statement is based on the
premise of the immutability of the national entity, the consequent
oneness of the State, as well as the continuity of the new constitution with the Meiji constitution. (According to the Cabinet,
the post-war constitution was "carried out in accordance with the
provisions of Article LXXIII of the Meiji Constitution.")[10]

On the question of the place of sovereignty in a country like
Japan, the Cabinet statement presents the views of the Minister of
State without Portfolio, Mr. Kanamori.

> The principle that sovereignty rests with the people raises the
> problem whether there has been a change or not in the position of
> sovereignty. If we inferred on the basis of a scholastic theory held
> hitherto which claims that sovereignty rests with the Throne, the

natural conclusion reached would be that sovereignty has been transferred to the people. Nevertheless, according to another view, sovereignty has always rested with the entire nation, the Emperor having been the controlling organ of national rights. This principle which
holds that sovereignty rests with the people is a thing to which the
people were hitherto not fully awake, having appeared in the form
of a theory which claimed that sovereignty rested with the State,
etc. The fact is that we have now entered into a period of awakening
to this point. Even in the past the Emperor's position was accompanied with an understanding on the part of the people, so that if we
looked upon the matter coolly on this basis, we would say that the
intrinsic qualities of the sovereignty resting with the people have
existed in the past. In short, the question is whether the change is
actual or apperceptive; but whichever it may be there is a change.
But as for myself I think the latter concept is the right one.

The foregoing is the Government's view concerning our national entity and sovereignty. . . .[11]

To a non-Japanese it seems fairly clear that the new constitution has brought about a fundamental change in the way of con-
ceiving the roles of the emperor, the people, and the state. Unlike
the Meiji constitution, the new one was not "graciously bestowed"
by the emperor; nor did it come from "the fulness of his power."
The emperor's position is derived from the will of the people.[12]
But of course it is up to the Japanese people what they will make of
the constitution. The emperor's position involves a kind of compromise between traditional and modern views. The basic rituals
of the imperial household are all Shinto, as in the past; and in
many of these the emperor himself is the central ritualist. In terms
of the theory of the new constitution, when the emperor engages
in these, it is only as a private individual. However, the *kami*
which he is worshipping are all of the Shinto *kami*, not just the
main ancestor of the imperial house, Amaterasu Omikami. There
is nothing in the constitution itself to prevent the Japanese people
from returning to the old ideology with its stress on the continuity
of the imperial line from the Divine Ages to the present.

The religious sentiments undergirding the Japanese state

may be vague, but they are more pervasive than those undergirding the constitution of the United States as felt by present-day
Americans. Mythology does not die by imperial rescript or by
legislative fiat. Under the veneer of even the most secular of states
there is a subtle mythology regarding race, clan, class, revolution,
purpose, destiny. Some mythologies are positively barbarous in
their effects as was the mythology that fed the masses of Germans
during the career of Hitler. Other mythologies can sustain a people
without making of them a threat to their neighbors. The mythology of Shinto was used by the Japanese militarists in such a way
as to make it diabolical in its social effects. But the mythology of
Christianity has also been used in ways destructive of peace,
harmony, and life itself. The crusading spirit dies slowly in some
cultures and religions, since the need to crusade seems to be tied
in with some basic insecurity in the crusader himself.

A part of the mythology of Shinto since very early times has
been the account of the heavenly origin of the imperial house.
Even in the midst of a war fought with modern weapons, the
emperor continued each year to participate in many Shinto rituals
concerned with the planting and harvesting of rice, the welfare
and prosperity of the nation. Man's need for some kind of mystic
identification cannot be denied. The question seems to be, what
form shall it take?

The ties that bind the imperial house to the Grand Shrine of
Ise, and to one of the main strands of Shinto thought and feeling,
are far deeper in their ramifications than are the ties that bind an
American president to the church of his choice. This holds true
even though a majority of the Japanese were to declare themselves
agnostic on all religious issues, for agnosticism to the Japanese is
a thing apart, of the head or of theory, whereas the feeling for that
which is "uniquely Japanese" is of the heart or of the blood, as it
were.

Legally and logically it is possible in Japan to separate
"church" and "state," allowing the emperor to carry on the rituals
of the imperial household as a private individual. But psycholog-
ically it is not as simple as that. In spite of the claims, made so
frequently, that the Japanese are a very irreligious people, the

fact remains that they are very emotional, and on their emotional side they have a feeling for the mystical that is often lacking in self-confessed agnostics and secularists in the West.

Outsiders are being unrealistic if they regard the legal disposition of the former connection between the state and Shinto as being the only issue of importance. It is important, but other issues or dimensions, vaguer and harder to get the Japanese themselves to discuss, are equally important. It is not a case of outsiders trying to tell the Japanese what they ought to do about it. This is an internal affair for the Japanese. But outsiders do have a responsibility of seeing to it that they do not misunderstand the complexity of the Japanese nature and society as blandly as they misunderstood it from the time of Perry down into the 1930's and 1940's.

What is the attitude of the Japanese people toward their emperor today? It is very difficult to get a satisfactory answer to this question. Many things which the Japanese think or feel, they are not inclined to express openly or too well before others, even their own countrymen. A priest of the Nishinomiya Shrine told me that the ordinary peasant still virtually worships the emperor. He gave this as an example of the force of the Shinto tradition. He commented that when the emperor visited various areas in the rural regions nearby, the people almost lay on the earth in front of him. He commented on the almost unavoidable need to bow low before the emperor which is felt by so many of the common people.

Just a few years after the close of the war a poll showed that a party advocating the abolition of the emperor system received less than 4 per cent of the votes cast. The party standing for the emperor system received over 96 per cent of the votes. Okubo, commenting on these figures, adds that in his opinion the Japanese national sentiment has not passed the test of any rational and logical criticism. He feels that the devotional feeling toward the imperial family is connected with the Japanese patriarchal type of society.[13]

In 1962 a poll was taken among Japanese Christian ministers and laymen regarding the emperor. It had to do with the question of changing the constitutional designation of the status of the emperor from "symbol" of the state to "sovereign head" of the state. (In 1957 the government had set up a Constitution Research Council to consider possible revision of the constitution. This Council suggested that the first article of the constitution, which says that the emperor is the "symbol of the State and of the unity of the people," is too illusory and hard to understand.) Ninety per cent of the persons replying to the survey sent out by the pollsters expressed opposition to changing the designation. This is hardly surprising since the Christians as a minority group have in the past often suffered at the hand of an unfriendly government.[14]

Another type of attitude toward the emperor is reflected in the comments of Yoshitaka Horie, a military critic and lecturer. The transcript of an interview with Mr. Horie was published in 1963 in an English-language journal, *Orient/West*. Asked about the relationship between the Japan Self Defense Force and the emperor, he replied:

> The JSDF do not want to discuss this subject in general. Some of the old types privately say that they don't like to be subordinate to the Prime Minister and the Superintendent-General of the Defense Agency; they seem to be dreaming of the "good old days," and to nourish friendly sentiments toward the Emperor.
>
> On the other hand, some of the young but already retired JSDF people are opposed to the Emperor's attitude after we lost the war; I heard that they complain privately that the Emperor ought to have done something as "leader of the country." After all, almost all of his Premiers and closest Generals and Admirals were either hanged or committed suicide. And 3,000,000 of his officers and men laid down their lives for him. Seven million family survivors still ask, "How could he have lived on without doing anything?"—whereas the concept of *bushidō*, the way of the samurai, implied that the leader ought to have committed *hara kiri* after his country was defeated.[15]

Another question put to Mr. Horie about some of the fundamental problems facing the Japan Self Defense Force brought this reply pertaining to the emperor.

Immediately after the turning point for us in August 1945, when we surrendered to the Allies, the Japanese people finally comprehended the true place of their country in the world. A number of feelings have since ensued. First, the end of mythological reliance upon the Emperor. Second, the exposure of our overestimation of the spirit and underestimation of material factors. Third, the old confidence in the Army and Navy turned to disappointment and hostility. Fourth, egotism replaced patriotism. . . . Efforts to use the role of the Emperor to advance the cause of Japanese military are no longer effective. In my opinion, the majority of the people—especially the new generation—will not be moved by mythology. As time goes by, the mythological power of the Emperor will in fact recede.[16]

What to do about the emperor and the emperor system is only one of the many problems with which Japan is grappling in the 1960's. The question of revision of the constitution is still very much alive. The question of a special status for the Grand Shrine at Ise will be discussed for some time to come, as well as the problem of special status for Yasukuni Shrine where the war dead are enshrined. How far public opinion on these questions will be an enlightened public opinion is any one's guess. In the past the destinies of Japan and her people have been decided by the relatively few at the top in numerous fields, usually referred to as "the big bosses." The Japanese hierarchical pattern is still strong, and the common people as a rule, in all fields, are still inclined to look "up" for answers (as well as security) instead of "out." So far as the government is concerned, traditionally the men who have controlled the government and the ideas they have held have been far more significant than the formal structure through which they have operated.[17]

Whether the Japanese people will really want democracy for themselves in practice is something yet to be decided. Under the new constitution democratic procedures are supposed to be followed in the functioning of the government. But feudalistic attitudes die out slowly, whether in politics, business, the family, or labor unions. The evidence in all of these areas is still inconclusive. Many of the younger Japanese have taken gladly to the idea of individual freedom and "the pursuit of happiness." But much of this is within the context of feudalistic or paternalistic patterns, as shown by the readiness with which the social and political radical of college days settles down to the conservative pattern once he enters a business firm where seniority is more important than ability and where responsibility is defined more by the ones above one than by an inner sense of responsibility.

All too many Japanese still think and feel that everything important happens, or should happen, in Tokyo. Centralization and the hierarchical patterns of thinking go hand in hand, reinforced by the desire to be near the centers of powers and influence. The fact that Tokyo may well strangle itself with its traffic, general congestion, overcrowding, exorbitantly high rents, is outweighed by the patterns of past feelings and tendencies. There is something deeply non-rational in this, stronger in the case of the Japanese than in other countries where the flight to the big urban centers is still in process. Whether Shinto as a living reality can survive in such an atmosphere is one of the crucial questions which members of the Association of Shinto Shrines are now facing.

CHAPTER ELEVEN

Shinto Today and Tomorrow

Over two decades ago an American scholar of Shinto wrote
of the Japanese citizen:

> . . . The old is ever there as a vital, all-pervading influence, funda-
> mentally conditioning his mentality and conduct and supplying a
> pattern to which all else must be accommodated. It permeates his
> home life, his agriculture, his business, his industry, his education,
> even his sports, and above all, his conception of the state and his
> duty to it.[1]

What he wrote as a statement of fact then should now be re-
phrased as a question. Is the old still there, as a vital all-pervading
influence? With the post-war generation it is still too soon to say.
Furthermore, the younger generation's concept of duty to the state
is still very clouded. Many of the students respond to slogans that
accuse the United States of making a satellite of Japan, but their
criticisms do not lead to constructive action. Socialism and communism, with their doctrinaire positions, for a few years have an
appeal for university students. But once the students get into
business firms, they settle down politically and socially somewhere to the right of center. Perhaps one reason that the left-wing
parties do not gain a larger following in Japan is that many of their
positions sound as though they were taken from textbooks written
long ago and far away.

In what way, then, will the old express itself in new Japan?
There is no great turning to Buddhism or to Christianity. Before
long, the newer religious movements will probably begin to taper
off in their growth, just as the somewhat older movements

(formerly known as "Sectarian Shinto") have become fairly static. Will Shinto take on renewed vitality under the leadership of some of its younger scholars and priests who have been abroad for study? Many of the Shinto priests are worried. Some are worried about the future of Shinto as a religious institution. Others are concerned about the need of modern Japanese man to find some way of combining his mechanical and scientific skills with aesthetic sensitivity and a capacity for continuing spiritual growth.

It is my opinion that Shinto does have something important to contribute to modern man's understanding of himself and his place in the universe. In the dialogue with science and the other religions and in confronting the problems posed by the machine and urbanization, Shinto also must be heard. In the modern world man has learned what he can do when he combines the skill of his mind and hands with the power of the machine. He can transform his world either for the common good or for total destruction. Which way that power will be used may well be decided within the next one hundred years. Whether any of the religious traditions of mankind will offer guidance in this process is an open question. Even where religions are prospering in the institutional and social sense, they are showing a singular lack of ability to redirect the imagination of men.

Probably the most significant challenge that the human race now faces is the task of merging the values of the past which are worth saving with new knowledge and techniques in such a way as to enhance the human spirit. In facing this task, Shinto is certainly in a no worse position than any of the major religions of mankind. In some senses it can be said to be in a more fortunate position in that it has been forced to take a serious look at itself because of the long years of the war, followed by the defeat and the Occupation. Shinto is burdened less by its failure (in the form in which it had been shaped since the Meiji period) than it would be had it been successful in that form. It is not burdened with voluminous scriptures, complicated systems of philosophy or theology, a comfortable priesthood enjoying worldly prosperity, or a dogmatic position to which it must cling. It is an intimate part of a culture which is a culture of feeling and tradition more than a culture of thinking and logic. This does not mean that Shinto thinkers will not have to do some solid, persistent thinking, but it will be the kind of thinking that takes human feelings more seriously than the theories of some modern intellectuals. For example, Shinto does not need to waste any energy talking about the salvation of the individual in some other world, for it cares not about some "other world." Here it is much closer to the attitude of the empirical scientist and secularist than it is to the usual theologian.

Shinto is an open-ended philosophical naturalism, and as such can speak more readily to modern seekers than the philosophies which appeal to irrational bases of authority—revealed books, church councils, or popes. It is in essential harmony with the approach of such men as William James, John Dewey, Henri Bergson, Henry Nelson Wieman, Alfred North Whitehead. It is something like this that some of the Shinto thinkers have in mind when they say Shinto is "the natural religion of man." The Shinto myth is naturalistic. There is no claim to revelation. It has no highly developed" doctrine of God," an asset in a century that has seen most of the doctrines of God fail to move men in their depths. There is no dualism in experience, no bifurcation of the universe in Shinto. There is no compulsive search for unity in theological theory. There is no appeal to naked power or omnipotence.

The crucial test of any religion or philosophy of life is what it does to men, not for them. What the religions of mankind have done to men is nothing that a historian of religion can rejoice over. It has made men subject to irrational authorities of one sort or another. It has often focused their attention on some life beyond the grave—a speculative concern which should never have been allowed to move into the center of the thinking and feeling of the common people. It has preached "goodness" without being able to display it, or the way to it, in relevant terms. It has often substituted moralism and puritanism for reflective morality. Lastly, it has given birth to its antithesis, anti-religion, which turns out to be just as dogmatic and brittle as that which it opposes—religion. If religion is the opiate of the people, so is anti-religion; they are blood-brothers under the skin.

Even after listing all these charges against the traditional religions, one is forced to admit that the religious dimension is an important part of the life of human beings. But how can this religious need or dimension in man express itself without succumbing to the dead hand of the past? Any religion which accepts the relativity and fallibility of all human perspectives—its own included—can avoid some of the dangers. Shinto certainly accepts its relativity. It makes no virtue of special religious practices or ascetic disciplines, yet it knows the discipline of simplicity of form and simplicity of desire. It recognizes that man is rooted in the soil and it makes no demand for eternal security beyond the grave or beyond the now.

Shinto is opposed to rigidity in any form. The Tokugawa period in Japanese life was hagridden by the past but it was Shinto that began to shape the destiny of a freer Japan. Unfortunately the Meiji government advisers became so enthusiastic over the industrial and military techniques of the West that they made of Shinto a device for promoting nationalism, one of the troublesome diseases of this age. But Shinto must not be identified with what went on in its name under the Meiji government and its successors up till 1945.

Shinto leaders are now free for the first time in a century to provide some critical guidelines for modern Japan as that nation seeks for some creative middle point between the extremes of "ancestor worship" and "worshipping the new." Much of the rigidity in Japanese life of the past several centuries can be traced to the influence of Confucian patterns of thought. The undue emphasis on rank, status, hierarchy, and obligation of the lower to the higher was essentially of Chinese Confucianist origin. Gradually it made its way into the very core of Japanese life, beginning at the upper levels of society. Almost every act, certainly all of the important ones from birth to death, became regulated by custom. The detailed laws and regulations of the Tokugawa regime were the end product of this kind of caste-structured society. Conformity to custom became almost second nature to most Japanese. The life of the many was increasingly controlled by the few at the top.

If the Japanese had learned long ago to be more critical of what they accepted from beyond their shores, they would have not become prisoners of their rulers to such a degree. Shinto leaders can help modern Japanese develop a capacity for sustained, thoughtful criticism. This is certainly in line with the basic methodology of Shinto, which knows no absolutes and which speaks for the aesthetic, intuitive side of man's nature. To accept the principle of fallibilism means to take seriously the habit of articulate criticism.

But canons of criticism do not emerge miraculously from "the group." They arise in the minds of individual persons who in turn invite or entice other individuals to enter into the continuing process of examination and re-education. There is no reason why Shinto cannot produce persons who can respect the past without clinging to it, combining what is best from that past with what is valuable in the present, and working for a better future with confidence.

The new generation in Japan is trying to define a *self* more than the pre-war generations. This is not easy in a society that has traditionally defined the self almost exclusively in terms of patterns of group obligations and dependencies. The Japanese word *amaeru* means to depend upon another's love, or to presume upon another's love. (Sometimes it is translated as "behaving like a spoilt child.") According to Dr. Takeo Doi this dependency pattern is "basic to individual Japanese psychology and is carried over into adult life and into all human relationships." It is this unsatisfied "urge to *amaeru*" which he finds to be the underlying dynamic of neurosis in Japan.[2]

The subordination of the individual to the group has so long been a part of the life of Japan that Japanese are hardly aware of it until they experience the contrast in a country more individually oriented. Recent studies indicate that even now Japan is essentially "familistic" in outlook rather than individualistic.[3] This finds expression in the feeling that the relationship between parent and child is more important than the relationship between husband and wife. Filial piety is the supreme virtue, which means, in effect, obedience. Because the individual is subordinated so completely to the group, it is hard for a sense of individual responsibility to emerge.

The general trend in all major societies today seems to be to depreciate the individual and emphasize the group, just as the stress falls more on security than on adventure. Japan faces this problem also, along with her traditional tendency to value the group more than the individual. But if man is not to betray his own spirit in its deeper dimensions, there must be persons who will speak up in behalf of *man the person*, the creator of values and the creator of that which is qualitatively significant in the group life.

Many Japanese have a habit of saying "Shikata-ga nai" ("It can't be helped") in situations where the world seems to have betrayed persons. As a waitress said of a young suicide, when she was talking with Laurens Van der Post, "The world betrays us all." But on this he commented: "It may be true that the world betrays us all. But I suspect that until the Japanese acquire in great measure the sense of responsibility for the daily betrayal of life that all men share, as well as the capacity to influence this responsibility, they will not be free of the darker aspects of their history and civilization."[4] But only persons who are really aware of themselves *as persons* can accept responsibility and seek constructive social outlets.

Modern man, in his aggravated search for security, runs the danger of trying to legislate everybody into the "group" and into the good life. This is part of the de-personalizing process at work in our world. Can he find a deeper quality of relatedness to his own inner potentialities as well as to nature, the matrix from which he comes? Shinto may be able to provide something of a corrective here, with its feeling for essential harmony and oneness with the cosmos. In place of the frenzied race to conquer nature or outer space, the focus might be changed to living harmoniously with nature, both inner and outer. Becoming further entranced with the products of our machines will heighten the neurotic patterns already present in our society, increasing the sense of restlessness and frustration.

And is not the Shinto intuition a sound one—that the meaning of life is to be found in the present, in the *now*? When people try to live too far ahead of themselves in the future or too far in the past, they tend to lose touch with the only place where creation or growth takes place. Man cannot know what purpose there may be in "the End" or in "the Beginning." But if he is alert he may learn something of what the purpose is for him, in the present. If Shinto can help people discover this in our times, it will have played an important part in the re-education of modern man.

Dates of Events During the Meiji Period
Directly Related to Shinto

Oct. 14, 1867	Last *Shōgun's* petition to be relieved of the government.
Dec. 9, 1867	Government restored to the Emperor Meiji.
Feb. 1868	*Jingi-ka* (Shinto Section) set up by government; title changed to *Jingi-jimukyoku* (Shinto Office).
April 5, 1868	A proclamation issued saying that "henceforth the government will be based on a return to the Imperial Rule of Jimmu Tennō."
April 6, 1868	Emperor Meiji proclaims the "Imperial Charter Oath of Five Articles."
April 9, 1868	Participation of Buddhist priests in Shinto shrines banned.
April 20, 1868	Edict separating Shinto and Buddhism.
May 1868	All Buddhist priests connected with Shinto shrines ordered to return to secular life. Those wanting to become Shinto priests must change their attire immediately.
June 11, 1868	*Jingi-kan* (Department of Shinto) replaces Shinto Office.
Nov. 30, 1868	Capital transferred from Kyoto to Tokyo.
	Hikawa Shrine dedicated as the tutelary shrine of Musashi Province, in which the new capital is located.
	Emperor Meiji issues an edict at Hikawa Shrine, indicating that the unity of religion and government (*saisei itchi*) shall be revived.
April 22, 1869	Emperor Meiji sends an official to worship at the grave of the first emperor, Jimmu Tennō.
April 25, 1869	Emperor Meiji, with government officials, performs a worship service in the Hall of Ceremonies in palace grounds to all the *kami*.
April 28, 1869	Shinto priests are ordered to let their hair grow.
April 29, 1869	All Shinto priests are put under the control of the Department of Shinto. The system whereby shrines were licensed by either the Yoshida or Shirakawa groups is ended. Shrines, as a consequence, are no longer dependent upon court nobles for favors.

June 1869	Yasukuni Shrine founded under name Tokyo Shō-kon-Sha (Souls-Inviting Shrine). Present name, enshrining those who gave their lives for the national cause, adopted in 1879. In June 1869, 3,588 people are enshrined. In 1964 2,500,000 enshrined.
August 5, 1869	Emperor Meiji visits the Department of Shinto to report to the Imperial ancestors the establishment of the national polity.
August 14, 1869	Department of Shinto given a position in the government higher than the Grand Council of State.
August 15, 1869	Government establishes Shinto propagators (sen-kyōshi) and announces the principle of proclaiming the "Great Teaching (Dai-kyō).
Oct. 17, 1869	Creation of an office called Caretaker of Imperial Mausolea (transferred almost immediately to the Department of Shinto).
Nov. 2, 1869	Government establishes the Office of Propaganda inside the Department of Shinto.
Jan. 18, 1870	Kami installed in new shrine opened for the work of the Office of Propaganda.
Feb. 3, 1870	Government holds a ceremony initiating the lectures to be given by the Shinto propagators. Imperial rescript issued proclaiming the "Great Teaching."
Feb. 14, 1870	Emperor visits the Department of Shinto and worships all the kami.
Nov. 1870	Department of Shinto petitions the throne to "decide general outlines of its policy and then issue specific regulations."
Feb. 1871	Government confiscates all temple lands.
June 1871	Government announces it will appoint the priests for all shrines.
Sept. 22, 1871	Jingi-shō (Shinto Ministry) replaces Department of Shinto.
Jan. 1872	Legislative Bureau suggests construction of shrine to Amaterasu within palace grounds, before which all important affairs of state are to be decided. Enunciates "Three Doctrines" of the "Great Teaching" (Dai-kyō).
April 21, 1872	Shinto Ministry abolished. Replaced by Kyōbu-shō (Department of Religion and Education). Set up system of "Edification and Guidance Officers" (kyōdō-

shoku). Both Shinto and Buddhist priests appointed to propagate the "Great Teaching." The "Three Doctrines" of the "Great Teaching" promulgated.

May 31, 1872

Government creates fourteen ranks of "national priests" to preach to the people.

Aug. 1872

All shrine priests made government officials.

June 3, 1873

Government issues explanatory statements for teaching the "Three Doctrines" of the "Great Teaching." Two sets of topics drawn up to be used as sermon material. Office of *Dai-kyō-in* established to carry out the details of the plan.

May 1875

Office of *Dai-kyō-in* abolished. *Shintō Jimukyoku* (Shinto Office) set up to provide communication between all of the shrines.

Government well on its way to abandoning the attempt to make Shinto a national *religion*.

Jan. 1877

Department of Religion and Education ceases operations. Functions transferred to the Bureau of Shrines and Temples in the Home Ministry. Government decides to be less aggressive in its religious policy.

System of "national priests" abolished. Appointment and dismissal of Buddhist priests transferred to the chief abbots of the Buddhist sects.

Feb. 11, 1889

Meiji Constitution bestowed upon the subjects.

Oct. 30, 1890

Imperial Rescript on Education issued.

April 24, 1900

Bureau of Shrines and Temples divided into two offices:
    (1) Office of Shrines
    (2) Office of Religions

Administratively shrines are separated from religions. Shrine Shinto declared to be not a religion; reverence for emperor and his ancestors obligatory on all Japanese.

Selected Bibliography

ANESAKI, MASAHARU. *History of Japanese Religion*. London: Routledge & Kegan Paul, Ltd., 1938.

ASTON, W. G. *Shinto: The Way of the Gods*. London: Longmans, Green, & Co., Ltd., 1905.

————. *Nihongi*. London: Allen & Unwin, 1956.

BEARDSLEY, R. K., and HALL, J. W. *Village Japan*. Chicago: University of Chicago Press, 1959.

BENEDICT, RUTH. *The Chrysanthemum and the Sword*. Boston: Houghton Mifflin Company, 1946.

BORTON, HUGH (ed.). *Japan*. Ithaca: Cornell University Press, 1951.

————. *Japan's Modern Century*. New York: The Ronald Press Company, 1955.

BUNCE, WILLIAM K. *Religions in Japan*. Rutland, Vt.: Charles E. Tuttle Co., Inc., 1960.

CHAMBERLAIN, BASIL H. *Things Japanese*. London: John Murray, Kelly & Walsh, 1905.

————. *Ko-Ji-Ki, or Records of Ancient Matters*. Kobe: Thompson, 1932.

"Contemporary Religions in Japan." Tokyo: International Institute for the Study of Religions, quarterly publication.

EMBREE, JOHN F. *Suye Mura—A Japanese Village*. Chicago: University of Chicago Press, 1939.

ERSKINE, WILLIAM H. *Japanese Customs—Their Origin and Value*. Tokyo: Kyo Bun Kwan, 1925.

————. *Japanese Festival and Calendar Lore*. Tokyo: Kyo Bun Kwan, 1933.

GAUNTLETT, J. O. (trans.). *Kokutai No Hongi, Cardinal Principles of the National Entity of Japan*. Cambridge: Harvard University Press, 1949.

GRIFFIS, WILLIAM E. *The Mikado: Institution and Person*. Princeton: Princeton University Press, 1915.

HALL, ROBERT K. *Shushin: The Ethics of a Defeated Nation*. New York: Columbia University Press, 1949.

HARING, DOUGLAS G., (ed.). *Japan's Prospect* (Chapter 7). Cambridge: Harvard University Press, 1946.

HEARN, LAFCADIO. *Kokoro: Hints and Echoes of Japanese Inner Life*. Boston: Houghton Mifflin Company, 1927.

————. *Japan: An Attempt at an Interpretation*. New York: The Macmillan Company, 1928.

HOLTOM, D. C. *The Japanese Enthronement Ceremonies*. Tokyo: Kyo Bun Kwan, 1928.

————. *The National Faith of Japan*. London: Routledge & Kegan Paul, Ltd., 1938.

————. *Modern Japan and Shinto Nationalism*. Chicago: University of Chicago Press, 1943.

Japan Advertiser, Enthronement edition. Tokyo: Fleisher, 1928.

KATO, GENCHI. "Japanese Phallicism," *Transactions of the Asiatic Society of Japan*, Vol. I (supplement), Series 2, 1924.

————. *A Study of Shinto*. Tokyo: Meiji Japan Society, 1926.

————. *What Is Shinto?* Tokyo: Japanese Government Railways, 1935.

KISHIMOTO, HIDEO (ed.) and HOWES, J. (trans.). *Japanese Religion in the Meiji Era*. Tokyo: Obunsha, 1956.

OKUBO, GENJI. *The Problems of the Emperor System in Postwar Japan*. Tokyo: Japan Institute of Pacific Studies, 1948.

ONO, SOKYŌ. *The Kami Way, An Introduction to Shrine Shinto*. Tokyo: International Institute for the Study of Religions, 1959; Rutland, Vt.: Charles E. Tuttle Co., Inc., 1963.

An Outline of Shinto Teachings, by the Shinto Committee for the Ninth International Congress for the History of Religions. Tokyo: Jinja Honchō, 1958.

PONSONBY-FANE, R. A. B. *Studies in Shinto and Shrines*, 1954; *Kyoto, the Old Capital of Japan*, 1956; *History of the Imperial House of Japan*, 1959; *Sovereign and Subject*, 1960; *Vicissitudes of Shinto*, 1963; *Visiting Famous Shrines in Japan*, 1964. All six volumes are published and sold by The Ponsonby Memorial Society, 58 Minamioji, Kamikamo, Kita-ku, Kyoto, Japan.

POWELL, PERCIVAL. *Occult Japan, or The Way of the Gods.* Boston: Houghton Mifflin Company, 1895.

Proceedings of the Ninth International Congress for the History of Religions, Tokyo, 1958. Tokyo: 1960.

REDESDALE, LORD. *Tales of Old Japan.* London: The Macmillan Company, 1928.

REISCHAUER, EDWIN O. *Japan, Past and Present.* Tokyo: Charles E. Tuttle Co., Inc., 1959.

"Religion and State in Japan," International Institute for the Study of Religions, Tokyo, September 1959.

"Religion and State in Japan," *Bulletin No. 7* of the International Institute for the Study of Religions, Tokyo, September 1959.

Religious Studies in Japan, by the Japan Association for Religious Studies. Tokyo: Maruzen, 1959.

SANSOM, G. B. *Japan, A Short Cultural History.* New York: Appleton-Century-Crofts, 1962.

SATOW, E., and FLORENZ, K. "Ancient Japanese Rituals," *Transactions of the Asiatic Society of Japan, Reprints,* Vol. II, December 1927.

STOETZEL, JEAN. *Without the Chrysanthemum and the Sword, A Study of the Attitudes of Youth in Post-War Japan.* New York: UNESCO, Columbia University Press, 1955.

TSUNODA, R., and DE BARY, KEENE. *Sources of the Japanese Tradition.* New York: Columbia University Press, 1958.

YANAIBARA, TADAO. *Religion and Democracy in Modern Japan.* Tokyo: Japan Institute of Pacific Studies, 1948.

Notes

CHAPTER ONE, VISIT TO A SHINTO SHRINE

1. The name of the *kami* enshrined at Suwa is Takeminakata-no-mikoto. The other subordinate *kami* of this shrine is the *kami* of Miho Shrine in Izumo. The name of the *kami* enshrined at Miho is Kotoshiro-nushi-no-mikoto. This feature of having subordinate *kami* group around the main enshrined *kami* is a feature often found in Shinto.

2. This Buddhist temple, Sakura-no-miya, is also called Sakura-daimyō-jin, and Sakura-ga-ike-ryōjin.

CHAPTER TWO, THE JAPANESE MYTH

1. The various Japanese accounts of the mythic beginnings occur in two major sets of writings, the *Kojiki* or *Records of Ancient Matters*, completed in 712 A.D., and the *Nihonshoki* or *Chronicles of Japan*, completed in 720 A.D. The narratives differ in details but our concern here is not with these differences. On the critical problem (sources, nature of the text, etc.), see B. H. Chamberlain, *Kojiki* (Kobe: Asiatic Society of Japan, 1932), Translator's Introduction, i-lxxxv; W. G. Aston, *Nihongi* (London: Allen & Unwin, Ltd., 1956), Introduction, ix-xx.

2. The Japanese term *mi-mi-o kakushi tamaiki* means "to hide oneself." The Japanese ordinarily do not think of *kami* as visible; they work without being seen.

3. Some accounts include at this point the birth of Amaterasu-Ōmikami, traditional ancestress of the imperial house and commonly known in the West as the Sun Goddess. However, the *Kojiki* is silent at this point. *See also* Ernest Satow, "Revival of Pure Shintau," *Transactions of the Asiatic Society of Japan, Reprints*, Vol. II, Dec. 1927. According to Hirata Atsutane, "Other countries were formed at a later period by spontaneous consolidation of sea foam and collection of mud in various localities. These foreign countries were produced by the power of the creator gods, but they were not begotten by Izanagi and Izanami. Nor did these countries give birth to the Sun Goddess; hence their inferiority. Japan lay directly opposite to the sun when it had sprouted upwards and separated from the earth. Thus Japan lies at the summit of the globe" (*ibid.*, p. 211).

4. George B. Sansom, "Some Problems of the Study of Japanese History," *Monumenta Nipponica*, Vol. I, No. 1, Sophia University, Tokyo, 1938, pp. 43–44.

5. *See* Aston, *Nihongi*, p. 5, notes 5, 6; p. 11, note 1. *Hashira* means "pillar," "column." *O-hashira* is the term applied to the end posts of a railing. Aston asks, "Is it a mere coincidence that *o-bashira*, male pillar, should contain the element *hashira* which is used as a numeral for deities?" He calls attention to the reed-shoot that was generated out of the mud, which was transformed into human shape, called Kuni-no Tokotachi-no-mikoto, and in another writing quoted in the *Nihongi* called Ama-no Tokotachi-no-mikoto, Heaven-of-Eternal-Stand.

6. Aston, *Nihongi*, p. 13.

7. Motoori Norinaga interpreted the Chinese characters, *hiruko*, as meaning "leech child," and many have followed him in this interpretation. Aston claims it should be translated as "Sun Male Child." Other scholars also interpret the word as meaning a child born of the sun. Genchi Kato says, "Hiruko is a sun-god, in contradistinction to the great Sun-Goddess, Amaterasu Ōmikami and her divine sister, Wakahirume-no-mikoto" (*A Study of Shinto* [Japan: Meiji Society], 1926, pp. 13–14, 69). The com-

pilers of the *Nihonshoki* (*Nihongi*) engaged in some fanciful speculations as to why this child and the subsequent one were defective (*see* Aston, *Nihongi*, pp. 15–17).

8. D. C. Holtom, *The National Faith of Japan* (London: Routledge & Kegan Paul, Ltd., 1938), pp. 103 ff.

9. *Ibid.*, pp. 106–107. See *Kojiki*, Vol. I, Sec. 8, pp. 37–40.

10. Hatsuo Okubo, *Norito Shiki Kōgi* (*Lectures on the Norito Ceremonies*), Vol. II, Osaka, 1908, fourth edition, pp. 3-4; cited in Holtom, *op. cit.*, p. 116.

11. The *Kujiki* account has these three *kami* all born of Izanagi and Izanami. *See* Post Wheeler, *The Sacred Scriptures of the Japanese* (New York: Abelard-Schuman Ltd., 1952), p. 20. See *Kojiki*, p. 49; J. W. T. Mason, *Spirit of Shinto Mythology* (Japan: Fuzambo, 1939), p. 49.

12. Post Wheeler comments, "Up to the close of the second world war it was suicidal for a Japanese scholar to suggest that the *kami* thus sent from the sky to the earth were spies and envoys despatched from the earlier base of the Sun Folk to Izumo, the earliest of whom were debauched by the local rulers" (Wheeler, *op. cit.*, p. 477, note 66).

13. *See* M. Anesaki, *History of Japanese Religion* (London: Routledge & Kegan Paul, Ltd., 1930), pp. 30–31.

14. *Nihongi*, Vol. II, No. 16, p. 77. The full name of Ninigi is very long and seems to imply plenty or fertility being carried

from heaven to earth. See *Kojiki*, Vol. 1, Sec. 33, note. 5.

15. Jimmu Tennō's name was Kami-Yamato-Ihare-Biko. Ihare is the name of a district in Yamato. Biko is the same as *hiko*, prince. Tennō is the Chinese pronunciation of the word meaning "emperor." The Japanese pronunciation is *sumera mikoto*, supreme majesty. *See* Aston, *Nihongi*, p. 109, note 1; Satow, "Rituals," *Transactions of the Asiatic Society of Japan*, Vol. VII, No. 2, p. 113.

16. The dates are not taken seriously by historians. Jimmu is more commonly placed in the first century B.C.

17. *Nihongi*, Vol. III, No. 3; also p. 131, note 1.

18. Aston, *Nihongi*, p. 131, modified by Holtom's rendering for readability. The character for "roof" also means "the universe." The eight cords or measuring tapes mean everywhere; that is, "the world under one roof." The "world" referred to here was of course a very small one.

19. Gishiwajinden, referred to by G. Kato, *op. cit.*, pp. 53–54. Cf. F. J. Horner, *Case History of Japan* (New York: Sheed and Ward, Inc., 1948), pp. 7–8.

20. William E. Griffis, *The Mikado: Institution and Person* (Princeton: Princeton University Press, 1915), p. 26.

21. Cf. Holtom, *op. cit.*, Ch. 9: Griffis, *op. cit.*, pp. 34–35; Boleslaw Szczesniak, "The Sumu-Sanu Myth," *Monumenta Nipponica*, Vol. X, Nos. 1–2, 1954, pp. 107–126.

CHAPTER THREE, SHINTO IDEAS OF *KAMI*

1. Chamberlain, *Kojiki*, 1932 edition, xix.

2. *Mienai karada* means a body which cannot be seen.

3. *See* Genchi Kato, *What Is Shinto?* Board of Tourist Industry, Japanese Government Railways, 1935, p. 24; W. G. Aston, "Shinto," *Transactions and Proceedings of the Japan Society*, London, Vol. VII, 1908, pp. 340 ff. Aston thinks this primal triad was not ancient in origin, and holds they are personifications of the Chinese male and female principles. But *see* Genchi Kato, *A Study of Shinto*, and M. Anesaki, *History of Japanese Religion* (Tokyo: Charles E. Tuttle Co., Inc., 1963), pp. 24–25.

4. As early as the time of the compilation of the *Nihonshoki*, the idea was already held that these *kami* were *kami* of creation.

5. The *musubi-no-kami* in the Shinto myth probably reflect the viewpoint of the thinkers or theologians. The *Nihonshoki's* ideas on creation myths were borrowed, in part, from China, according to most Japanese scholars. Chamberlain suggests they may have been the work of individual priests (Chamberlain, *Kojiki*, lxxiv).

6. Kato, *A Study of Shinto*, pp. 52–54, *See also* D. C. Holtom, *Modern Japan and Shinto Nationalism*, University of Chicago Press, 1943, pp. 62-65; W. K. Bunce, *Re-*

ligions in Japan (Tokyo: Charles E. Tuttle Co., Inc., 1955), pp. 100-101.

7. G. Kato and Hoshino's English translation of the *Kogoshūi*, third edition, 1926, p. 46.

8. A catechism of the Taisha-Kyō, the religious teaching division of the Izumo Shrine under the Meiji government, says: "As Great Land Master is the ruler of the hidden world, he has in charge the rulership of the spirits. The place to which spirits go after their death differs according to their virtues and demerits. Some rise to the Sky. Some descend into the Earth. Others must follow the path to the Land-of-Roots.... But as all these must dwell in some portion of the hidden world, it behooves us to put trust in Great Land Master, the hidden world's ruler" (cited in Wheeler, *op. cit.*, pp. 466–467).

9. *Nihongi*, Vol. I, p. 316.

10. *Nihongi*, Vol. I, p. 347.

11. See K. Florenz, *Ancient Japanese Rituals*, p. 102 (cited in Mason, *op. cit.*, p. 79).

12. *Nihongi*, Vol. I, p. 281.

13. *Taittriya Upanishad* 2.2.

14. Holtom says that: "The fact that *mata* signifies groin, thigh, crotch, or fork may possibly point to the original association which, under the operation of the principles of imitative magic, made the human Crotch-Kami also a Road-Fork-Kami" *(Monumenta Nipponica*, Vol. III, No. 2, p. 358).

One other passage in the mythic account of Izanagi's flight from the underworld suggests phallic connotations. At one point Izanagi holds back the malignant powers by hurling peaches at them. This suggests some kind of female sex magic. Like the phallus, the peach carries the resources of life, health, and vigor. (Belief in the magical power of the peach came to Japan from China, apparently.) Holtom adds that the peach serves as a mighty prophylactic

against the demonic powers that bring sickness and misfortune, the powers attributed to the peach lying in its appropriateness in representations of the female sex organ (*op. cit.*, p. 365). See *Nihongi*, p. 30; *Kojiki*, pp. 43–44.

15. *Futamata* means forked; *mata* also means groin or crotch. When a different name is ascribed to a *kami*, it usually means the *kami* has a different function. According to the account in the *Kojiki*, Road-Fork-Kami was born when Izanagi threw down his staff at the time of his purification after leaving the underworld. The name given to the staff, Tsuki-tatsu-funado-no-kami, means "Thrust - Erect - Come - Not - Place - Kami." The "thrust erect" would seem to refer to the way in which the objects were erected at the roadside. At certain periods in Japanese history there was a practice of erecting phallic images by the wayside and at crossroads, to ward off evils. There is one reference to such in the *Kogoshūi*. How much of this derived from indigenous Folk Shinto or how much from some "new religion" reflecting possible Hindu influence, is a matter of conjecture among the scholars at the present time.

16. See "Yachimata-hiko and Yachimata-hime," *Shinto Daijiten*, Vol. III, p. 367. See Holtom, *op. cit.*, p. 359; Kato, *A Study of Shinto*, pp. 31, 171-172.

17. Donald L. Philippi, *Norito, A New Translation of the Ancient Japanese Ritual Prayers* (Tokyo: The Institute for Japanese Culture and Classics, 1959), No. 13, p. 53. Cf. Holtom, "Meaning of Kami," *Monumenta Nipponica*, Vol. III, No. 1, 1940, pp. 1–27; No. 2, pp. 329–413. See the *Kojiki* account of the barrier stones set up by Izanagi, Vol. I, Sec. 9. Cf. Kato, *A Study of Shinto*, p. 31.

18. Quoted in Kato, *A Study of Shinto*, p. 186.

19. *Ibid.*, p. 38.

CHAPTER FOUR, THE FESTIVALS OF SHINTO

1. The oldest reference in which the form of the ancient rituals can be seen comes from the Nara period, the *Yōrōyō*, the basic law of policy and administration. For a list

of the names of the festivals, see *Engishiki*, *Kokushi Taikei*, Vol. XIII, p. 92, cited in Kato, *A Study of Shinto*, pp. 101-103.

2. *Ibid.*

3. *Norito* 13, in Philippi, *Norito*, pp. 53–54.

4. The *Jingi-ryō* and the *Engishiki*, in the Heian period and after. After the Meiji period, in the *Tōkyoku-rei.*

5. *See* Kato, *A Study of Shinto*, p. 177. The government order of the eighth century says, "In the Shinto ceremonies at night men and women get drunk and are licentious with one another, to the injury of public morals. Henceforward Shinto ceremonies should be conducted by day, and not by night" (*Ruijū-Sandai-Kyaku*, Vol. XIX; *Kokushi Taikei*, Vol. XII, p. 988).

6. Motoori interpreted the word *himorogi* as *moro, muro,* or *heya* = room, and *gi* or *ki* = tree; *hi* stands for something mysterious; here it means *kami.* At Ō-Miwa Shrine in Nara-ken where there is no inner sanctuary, the mountain itself being considered sacred as the *go-shintai*, the mountain is called *mi-moro-yama.*

7. *Nihongi*, Vol. II, No. 22, pp. 81–82.

8. Saigyo Hoshi (1118–1190), quoted in R. K. Hall, *Kokutai-no Hongi* (Cambridge: Harvard University Press, 1949), p. 141.

9. *See* Philippi, *Norito.* After the Meiji Restoration, the government sought to standardize the *norito*, indicating which ones were to be used on which occasions. These prescribed rituals have not, of course, been in force since 1945. The shrines are free to use what prayers they wish, whenever they feel it appropriate to do so.

10. *Nihongi*, Vol. II, No. 23, p. 83; *Kojiki*, Vol. I, pp. 130–131. *See* Chamberlain's note, p. 130, note 20. *See also* D. C. Holtom, *Modern Japan and Shinto Nationalism*, p. 57; W. K. Bunce, *Religions in Japan*, pp. 2–3; Hanso Tarao, "Symbols of Sovereignty," *The Japan Advertiser*, Enthronement Edition, Tokyo, 1928, pp. 63–65.

11. *See* Kato, *op. cit.*, pp. 108–109; R. A. B. Ponsonby-Fane, *Imperial House of Japan* (Kyoto: Ponsonby Memorial Society, 1959), pp. 31–32.

12. The replica of the sword was lost at the time of the fight against the Taira clan in the battle of Dan-no-Ura in 1185. A second replica was made, and then a third which was given to the emperor from the province of Ise in 1210.

13. *Jinnō Shōtōki*, Vol. I, p. 20, quoted in Kato, *op. cit.*, pp. 149–150.

CHAPTER FIVE, THE EMPEROR AND THE GREAT FESTIVAL OF NEW FOOD

1. *Nii* means new; *name* means food. *Shinjō* also means new food. *O* or *dai* means big. This is the explanation which Motoori Norinaga made.

2. In the *Dai-hō-ryō*, the law of the Nara period, there is a section on Shinto called the *Jingi-ryō.* In this section both the *Dai-jō-sai* after the enthronement and the ordinary annual *Dai-jō-sai* (today's Niiname-sai) are described as *Dai-jō-sai.* However, at some point a distinction was made. In the *Nihonshoki* (a book older than the *Dai-hō-ryō*), the word *Niiname-sai* (as well as *Shinjō-sai*) appears; so the term is older than the *Dai-hō-ryō.* *Niinae-no-matsuri* is another way of pronouncing the same characters.

3. The public enthronement ceremony seems to have started after the Taika Reform in the Nara period, using the occasion of the *Dai-jō-sai.* In the *Kogoshūi* two ritu- als are described, *Dai-jō-sai* and an enthronement ceremony. The author of the *Kogoshūi* wrote the history of the first emperor, Jimmu, as though there were both a public enthronement ceremony and *Dai-jō-sai* at that time. When we consult a book written in the beginning of the Heian period on *Dai-jō-sai*, we find that the ceremony closely resembled the enthronement ceremony of China, such things as costumes, flags, and decorations being almost the same as Chinese ones.

4. From about the middle of the Heian period the eastern country was settled at Ōmi-no-kuni, an area now a part of present-day Kyoto in the north. The other country or area was Tamba or Bitchū in Okayama-ken. Hence the divination became the way of choosing the *gun* or county within the larger area or *kuni* (country). At the *Dai-jō-sai* of the emperor Meiji, the rule that

the *Yuki-no-Kuni* was to be to the east of the capital and the *Suki-no-Kuni* to the west was not followed. The former was located in Yamanashi-ken and the latter in Chiba-ken.

5. *See* D. C. Holtom, *The Japanese Enthronement Ceremonies* (Tokyo: Kyo Bun Kwan, 1928), pp. 117–118.

6. *Ibid.*, pp. 109–112. *See* Zoe Kincaid, "Ceremonies of Accession," *Japan Advertiser*, Enthronement Edition, Tokyo, 1928, p. 30.

7. Holtom, *The Japanese Enthronement Ceremonies*, pp. 121–122.

CHAPTER SIX, PURIFICATION IN SHINTO

1. *Nihongi*, Vol. I, No. 27, p. 32. It is this *kami* that is worshipped at the Outer Shrine at Ise.

2. *See* Philippi, *Norito*, note 13.

3. *Ibid.*, pp. 47–48. Another translation of this *norito* is included in the text of the *Kokutai-no Hongi*, pp. 132–133.

4. *Nihonshoki-Sanso*, Vol. II, p. 112, quoted in Kato, *A Study of Shinto*, p. 165.

5. *Kokushi Taikei*, Vol. VII, p. 487, quoted in Kato, *op. cit.*, p. 163.

6. *Daijingū Sankeiki, Gunsho Ruijū*, Vol. I, p. 982, quoted in Kato, *op. cit.*, p. 166.

7. For a detailed treatment *see* Professor Kosei Ando, *Nihon-no Miira* (Tokyo: Mainichi Press, 1961). For a treatment in English *see* Professor Ichiro Hori, "Self-Mummified Buddhas in Japan, An Aspect of the Shugendō Sect," *History of Religions*, Vol. 1, No. 2 (Winter 1961), pp. 222–242.

8. Hori, *op. cit.*, p. 224.

CHAPTER SEVEN, ETHICS IN SHINTO

1. Sokyō Ono, "Shinto and Ethics," in *An Outline of Shinto Teachings* (Tokyo: Jinja Honchō, Kokugakuin University, Institute for Japanese Culture and Classics, 1958), p. 27.

2. Hirata Atsutane, *Koshiden*, Vol. VI; Yamada Takao, *Hirata Atsutane*. See *Kojiki*, Vol. I, Sec. 10, p. 49.

3. M. Anesaki, *Mythology of All Races*, p. 237; "Tama" in *Basic Terms of Shinto*, Institute for Japanese Culture and Classics, Tokyo, 1958.

4. *Kogoshūi*, p. 27; *Nihongi*, Vol. I, p. 83; *Kojiki*, p. 109.

5. *See* Kato, *A Study of Shinto*, p. 34; *Manyōshū*, Vol. V.

6. Many of the scholars of the Tokugawa period, including Motoori, were inclined to regard these four as aspects of the same soul or spirit. However, Kato claims that the ancient Japanese, like early peoples everywhere, believed that each individual had several souls (*op. cit.*, pp. 32–33).

7. Only under Chinese influence did the Japanese begin to give much thought to the concept of the soul. The Chinese conception of the soul was based on the Yin-Yang theory. The soul was composed of two factors, one closely related to the world of matter, the other subtle and aerial. "The destinies of these two factors were determined partly by the nature of the person to whom they belonged, and partly by the place of burial. But these ideas did not influence Japanese folk-lore so much as the elaborate teachings of Buddhism on the nature of transmigration" (Anesaki, *op. cit.*, p. 238)

8. R. C. Armstrong, *Just Before the Dawn, The Life and Works of Ninomiya Sontoku* (New York: The Macmillan Company, 1912), Garrett Droppers, "A Japanese Credit Association and Its Founder," *Transactions of the Asiatic Society of Japan*, 21, 1893, p. 82, cited in R. Bellah, *Tokugawa Religion* (Glencoe: The Free Press), p. 129.

9. Hajime Nakamura, "Some Features of the Japanese Way of Thinking," *Monumenta Nipponica*, Vol. XIV, No. 3–4, pp. 31—72. He points out similar tendencies in Jōdo Shū (Pure Land Buddhism). Mundane existence and Nirvana are one and the same. He quotes Nichiren's letter to a warrior: "Man and woman in copulation chant Namu Myōhō Renge-kyō, that is exactly what we mean with 'The affliction is nothing but enlightenment,' and 'Mundane existence is

nothing but Nirvana' " (*ibid.*, p. 40).

10. Lafcadio Hearn, *Japan: An Attempt at an Interpretation* (New York: The Macmillan Company, 1928), p. 112.

11. *Nihongi*, Vol. III, No. 30, p. 131.

12. Quoted in Hall, *Kokutai-no Hongi*, p. 112.

13. Ponsonby-Fane, *Imperial House of Japan*, p. 5.

14. *Honchō Monzui*, Vol. XIII, p. 1, in Kato, *What Is Shinto?* p. 45; Kato, *A Study of Shinto*, p. 163.

15. *Chucho-Jijitsu*, in Kato, *What Is Shinto?* p. 45.

16. Interview with Professor Anzu of Kokugakuin University, July 3, 1961.

CHAPTER EIGHT, THE REVIVAL OF SHINTO AND THE MEIJI RESTORATION

1. Quoted in Hall, *Kokutai-no Hongi*, p. 130.

2. Hideo Kishimoto (ed.) and John Howes (trans.), *Japanese Religion in the Meiji Era* (Tokyo: Obunsha, 1956), p. 27.

3. There was also a conflict of loyalties around the shogunate itself, with two contenders for the head position of *shōgun*, or military boss, and two competing factions in the Tokugawa party. This struggle was to continue till 1858 as a background to the struggles over what to do about the foreigners who wanted to open trade with Japan. See Hugh Borton, *Japan's Modern Century* (New York: The Ronald Press Company, 1955), pp. 39–40; Robert K. Hall, *Shushin: The Ethics of a Defeated Nation* (New York: Columbia University Press, 1949), pp. 23 ff.

4. Borton, *op. cit.*, p. 55.

5. The last *shōgun's* petition to the emperor was written on October 14, 1867.

6. Hugh Borton points out that while the emperor's opinion was sought out and followed in times of crisis, "the key to obtaining Imperial sanction to any policy was to obtain previous approval from his closest advisers. Hence . . . the importance of Emperor Meiji in history was the manner in which his chief ministers were able to use his name and his position to obtain acceptance of their policies" (*Japan's Modern Century*, pp. 89–90).

7. Quoted in Hall, *Shushin: The Ethics of a Defeated Nation*, p. 28.

8. *Ibid.*, pp. 29–30.

9. Shozo Kono, *Jingishi Gaiyō (Outline of Shinto History)*, Tokyo, 1927, p. 43; quoted in Holtom, *Modern Japan and Shinto*

Nationalism, p. 5.

10. Hall, *Kokutai-no Hongi*, pp. 138–139.

11. Kishimoto and Howes, *Japanese Religion in the Meiji Era*, p. 53.

12. *Ibid.*, pp. 45–46.

13. *Ibid.*, pp. 67–70.

14. *Ibid.*, p. 71.

15. *Ibid.*, p. 73.

16. *Ibid.*, p. 92.

17. Hall, *Shushin: The Ethics of a Defeated Nation*, pp. 42–43.

18. Holtom, *Modern Japan and Shinto Nationalism*, p. 9. See Borton, *Japan's Modern Century*, pp. 128 ff, for a good discussion of the centralized monarchy, the part played by Ōkuma and Itō, the influence of Bismarck, and Prussian concepts and their effect on the organization of the system of education after 1880.

19. Hall, *Shushin: The Ethics of a Defeated Nation*, p. 37.

20. Borton, *Japan's Modern Century*, pp. 177–178.

21. See Bunce, *Religions in Japan*, pp. 30–31.

22. Holtom, *Modern Japan and Shinto Nationalism*, p. 80, gives the quotation from Fujisaku Maru, *Kokutai-no Hongi Seikai* ("Commentary on the Fundamental Principles of the National Structure"), Tokyo, 1937, pp. 63–64.

23. Quoted by Y. Haga, "Spirit of Japan," *Transactions and Proceedings of the Japan Society*, Vol. XV (1917), p. 125.

24. Quoted in Hall, *Kokutai-no Hongi*, p. 105.

25. Quoted in *Kokumin Dōtoku Jō yori Mitaru Jinja*, Shintō Kōza, Vol. II, Tokyo, 1929, pp. 102 ff.

CHAPTER NINE, BACKGROUND TO DISASTER: 1912-1945

1. Shozo Kono, "Kannagara-no Michi," *Monumenta Nipponica*, Vol. III, No. 2, pp. 369-391.

2. *Nihongi*, Vol. III, No. 3, pp. 110-111.

3. Fukusaku Yasubumi, "Kokumin Dō-toku jō yori Mitaru Jinja." ("The Shrines Considered from the Standpoint of National Morality"), Society for the Investigation of Shinto, Lectures on Shinto, quoted by Holtom, *National Faith of Japan*, pp. 140-141. See *National History for Ordinary Primary Schools*, Vol. I, Ch. 1, quoted in Holtom, *op. cit.*, p. 131. Ponsonby-Fane, *The Imperial Family and Shinto, Transactions and Proceedings of the Japan Society*, Vol. XXVII (1930), pp. 47 ff.

4. Quoted from Yamaga Sokō (1622-1685), in Hall, *Kokutai-no Hongi*, p. 129.

5. Cf. Borton, *Japan's Modern Century*, p. 331.

6. In February, 1936, some 1,400 troops of the First Division of the army seized control of part of downtown Tokyo, assassinated several high officials, and then surrendered three days later because of an imperial command. Thirteen of the officers involved were executed in July of 1936 and the War Ministry had to dissociate itself from the ideas advocated by this group. However, the trend to rely more and more on the armed forces increased. As Borton says: "No group, economic or political, challenged the basic policy of expansion on the continent of Asia. The Army alone had a plan. It advocated the formation of a bloc composed of Japan, Manchukuo, and North China to strengthen the country economical-ly and to protect it from attack from the Soviet Union. In the absence of anything better and lacking a liberal, non-military tradition, the people followed" (*ibid.*, p. 341).

7. Bunce, *Religions in Japan*, pp. 37-38. Of the Japanese Christians he writes: "In the early decades of the modern era, Christians remained aloof from Shrine worship, but, in 1940, they participated fully, even to the extent of sending representatives to report at Ise Shrine regarding ecclesiastical activities. For some time, the Catholic Church refused to participate in Shrine worship, but, finally, on the basis of the government's declaration that shrines were not religious, permission was given, and 'shrine obeisance' by Catholic bodies became common. Only a few Christian groups refused to participate in such worship. The others permitted themselves to drift with the nationalistic current flowing so strongly through Japanese life." Cf. Holtom, *Modern Japan and Shinto Nationalism*, pp. 82, 102-103.

8. See Hall, *Kokutai-no Hongi*, p. 10.

9. *Ibid.*, pp. 50, 54.

10. *Ibid.*, p. 59.

11. *Ibid.*, p. 71.

12. *Ibid.*, pp. 73, 75-76, 80.

13. *Ibid.*, pp. 82-83.

14. *Ibid.*, pp. 100, 132.

15. *Ibid.*, p. 161.

16. *Ibid.*, pp. 166-167.

17. Borton, *op. cit.*, p. 321.

18. Quoted in Holtom, *Modern Japan and Shinto Nationalism*, p. 10.

CHAPTER TEN, SHRINE SHINTO SINCE 1945

1. See Hall, *Kokutai-no Hongi*, pp. 45-46: "United States policy on Shinto was first publicly enunciated in a radio broadcast by a Department of State official, John Carter Vincent. . . . On October 13, 1945, the Secretary of State communicated the pertinent portion of the Vincent broadcast to the Headquarters of the Supreme Commander for the Allied Powers with the statement that it was a paraphrase of a State, War, and Navy Coordinating Committee (SWN-CC) paper not yet received by Occupation Headquarters." The paraphrase stated: "Shintoism insofar as it is a religion of individual Japanese is not to be interfered with. Shintoism, however, insofar as it is directed by the Japanese Government and is a measure enforced from above by the

Government, is to be done away with. People would not be taxed to support National Shinto and there will be no place for Shintoism in the schools. Shintoism as a State Religion, National Shinto, that is, will go. Our policy on this goes beyond Shinto. The dissemination of Japanese Militarists and ultra-Nationalistic ideology in any form will be completely suppressed and the Japanese Government will be required to cease financial and other support of Shinto establishments."

2. *Ibid.*, p. 45; comment by editor, R. K. Hall.

3. *See* Bunce, *Religions in Japan*, pp. 166–168.

4. "Japan as of Today," *Japan Magazine*, Vol. II, No. 2 (Winter 1958), p. 12.

5. The official English translation of this rescript is given in full in Hall, *Kokutai-no Hongi*, pp. 196–197.

6. *Kokutai-no Hongi*, p. 46.

7. For some of the background source material *see* F. C. Jones, H. Borton, and B. R. Pearn, *The Far East, 1942–1946* (London: Oxford University Press, 1955), Appendix 12: "The McArthur Directive on Political and Other Liberties, providing for religious freedom through the abrogation of the Religious Body Law of 1939 which was still in effect"; Appendix 17: "Criteria for the Adoption of a New Japanese Constitution, 13 May, 1946"; Appendix 19: "Basic Principles for a New Japanese Constitution, 2 July, 1946"; Appendix 21: "Constitution of Japan."

8. *See* Bunce, *op. cit.*, p. 171; Japan Magazine, *op. cit.*, p. 12.

9. Hall, *Kokutai-no Hongi*, Appendix 7, pp. 198–199.

10. *Ibid.*, p. 199.

11. *Ibid.*, pp. 199–200. Cf. Genji Okubo, *The Problems of the Emperor System in Post-War Japan*, The Japan Institute of Pacific Studies, 1948, pp. 58–59; 65.

12. *See* Peter J. Herzog, S.J., "Political Theories in the Japanese Constitution," *Monumenta Nipponica*, Vol. VII, Nos. 1–2 (Jan. 1951).

13. Okubo, *op. cit.*, pp. 76, 83, 87.

14. *Japan Christian Activity News*, Published by the Commission on Public Relations of the National Christian Council of Japan, Dec. 1, 1961; March 1, 1962.

15. Interview with Yoshitaka Horie in the *Orient/West*, Vol. VIII, No. 4, July-August 1963, pp. 54–58. Above quotation from p. 56.

16. *Ibid*, p. 58. Some of Mr. Horie's other comments, if valid, should give American policy-makers pause. "Most of the people view JSDF as Japan's 'diplomatic obligation' to the United States–the latter's 'puppet troops,' in fact. Few feel that JSDF would ever play a decisive role in determining Japan's fate.... To be frank, I believe that the people of Japan would cooperate with the Free World only to the extent of the power of America's military might. The feelings which I mentioned before are widespread, and it might be next to impossible to expect from the Japanese people any strong bonds for defending their own country. In other words, it is doubtful that Japan could really serve as a Free World 'pillar' in Asia."

17. Borton, *Japan's Modern Century*, p. 463.

CHAPTER ELEVEN, SHINTO TODAY AND TOMORROW

1. Holtom, *Modern Japan and Shinto Nationalism*, p. 2.

2. Takeo Doi, "Jibun to Amaeru-no Seishin Byōri," in *Seishin Shinkei Gaku Zasshi*, 1960–1961, pp. 149–162, quoted in Lifton, p. 185.

3. *See* T. O. Wilkinson, "Family Structure and Industrialization in Japan." *American Sociological Review*, Vol. XXV, No. 5 (Oct. 1962), p. 680.

4. Laurens Van Der Post, *Holiday*, Oct. 1961, p. 131.

Index